Profit Opportunities in
Real Estate Investments

Profit Opportunities in Real Estate Investments

Calvin L. Greenberg

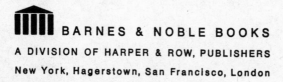
BARNES & NOBLE BOOKS

A DIVISION OF HARPER & ROW, PUBLISHERS

New York, Hagerstown, San Francisco, London

First BARNES & NOBLE BOOKS edition published 1978

ISBN: 0-06-463470-1

79 80 81 82 10 9 8 7 6 5 4 3

Dedicated to the feminine influence,
which helped—considerably.

> Carol
> Estelle
> Paulette

Calvin L. Greenberg

Calvin L. Greenberg is Chairman of the Board of Balter & Greenberg, Inc., one of the nation's leading real estate investment firms. He has been engaged in real estate as an investor, builder and broker for over 25 years.

Mr. Greenberg is a member of the National Association of Realtors, the Long Island Real Estate Board, the National Association of Real Estate Appraisers and the New York State Society of Real Estate Appraisers.

He has written hundreds of articles on real estate and is the author of *How to Become a Successful Store Leasing Broker,* published by Prentice-Hall, Inc. Mr. Greenberg holds a masters degree in business administration.

What This Book Will Do For You

This book covers the most popular and profitable classes of investment properties. It also explains the various techniques used to achieve individual tax savings and earn maximum profits. These techniques produce profits for all types of investment properties. Furthermore, these methods may be used by anyone who reads this book.

Chapter 1. Divulges how to develop the heart of the investment business; how to develop financing skills as an investor. The various types of loans are discussed, and you are told exactly where to apply when you need a mortgage. The chapter provides a storehouse of knowledge plus important techniques that will be an extraordinary aid in solving financial problems.

Chapter 2. This chapter reveals an absolutely fantastic formula. A formula that permits even a complete novice to be able to determine the return on equity that you are entitled to receive. The formula also creates instant knowledge of market conditions.

Chapter 3. This is an intelligent approach toward getting the highest return on your investment—with safety. Also, how to determine if the yield offered is a true return. How to take advantage of bargains in panic sales.

Chapter 4. The book tells how to develop the use of depreciation to maximum advantage. Outlined are the government-given gifts of tax shelter.

Chapter 5. This chapter makes known new and better ways to finance properties through the little known wrap-around mortgage. It explains how to make seemingly impossible deals through the use of the fabulous wrap-around. Actual instances of the wrap-around in use are carefully explained.

Chapter 6. I'll tell you when to liquidate, at a profit, and when to buy in order to make a profit. Also, how to obtain free appraisals of your property.

Chapter 7. The book offers a system that reveals the profit increments available in investment in *net leases.* Net leases are explained in detail. Types of locations, buildings and locations are covered. Of great value is a formula that reveals what return on your money you should get.

Chapter 8. I explain the various tax pitfalls and suggest safeguards to avoid these pitfalls. How to legally avoid various taxes applicable to real estate. Methods of using tax shelter, tax free trades, installment sales, non-taxable income, deferred taxes, division of income, Keogh Plan and others.

Chapter 9. I examine hidden profits and show you how to find them and how to create wealth through *office buildings.* Actual case histories are followed step-by-step. Rental patterns and trends are examined. Vacancy causes, outmoded buildings, meaning of plot sizes, rentable area, refinancing, income estimates, expense estimates, leasing— all the pertinent points are covered.

Chapter 10. Examines and explains how to pyramid with *one family* dwellings. How to buy for the future. How a good buy in a one family dwelling can create a secure future. What it takes to invest.

Chapter 11. This chapter explains how to use *leaseholds* as an untapped source of wealth. How to apply the leasehold method to any type of real estate. How to control land without buying the property. How to actually apply the leasehold—one of real estate's more sophisticated tools.

Chapter 12. The book shows how to reap big profits from *co-operative apartments.* Comparison with condominiums. Advantages of co-op ownership. Financing, pitfalls, avoiding excessive management fees, 213 financing and other pertinent aspects are delved into.

Chapter 13. The book shows money-making secrets for investing in *sandwich leases.* How to make money investing in your "own back yard." Big money is not necessary—nor is travel. Tells what a sandwich lease is. How to use a sandwich lease. Why sandwich can create big money for you.

Chapter 14. I show remarkably easy ways to invest in a secure future through *taxpayer properties.* How to rate taxpayers. Tips on taxpayer financing. Reveals which areas are poor risks. Correct methods of determining true expenses. How to avoid "bargains."

Chapter 15. I explain how to get your share of the *shopping center* market. Various types of centers are investigated. How to structure leases. Determining realistic expenses. How the money is made in shopping centers.

Chapter 16. This shows how to use my formula for multiplying your assets through *marginal properties.* How to go into "blighted areas" and turn substantial profits. Many types of properties in rundown areas may be quickly converted to substantial profits.

Chapter 17. The book tells how to use present tenancy to produce big profits—without increasing rentals. It shows how to create your own bargains. Management tips for increasing your profits are carefully explained.

Chapter 18. The book illustrates how to obtain unusual advantages through the use of *leverage.* Types of properties that lend themselves to leverage financing. What immediate results are created through leverage.

Chapter 19. The book explains how to own *condominiums.* How to sell condominiums. How to buy condominiums. All of the secrets carefully explained. Tax benefits, financing benefits, and overall benefits of condominiums.

Chapter 20. The book tells you how to utilize little known methods for creating tremendous profits through operation, management and sale of older run down buildings. How to have liability insurance at no cost. Amount of time necessary to manage an old, run down building.

Chapter 21. This chapter deals with today's go-go properties—the *drive-in*. It covers buying, selling, operating and packaging drive-ins. Explains correct yields for different type AAA-1 tenancy. Drive-in bargains are hidden and you must know where to look.

Chapter 22. The secrets of buying and selling *land* are closely covered. How to estimate if the price is "right." How land is re-used.

A Word From The Author

The real estate investment profession—the buying, trading and selling of investment property—is the greatest, biggest business in the world. People are involved in this enterprise in every civilized center throughout the world. There is a greater quantity of money produced in realty investment buying and selling than in any other field. Consequently, we know that we are dealing with a genuinely huge business, one that has the ability to earn anyone fantastic riches. I plan to make known in this book how you may achieve all this.

Very Nearly Anyone Can Qualify

Producing money in the investment field is not luck. Money can best be made through know-how. Under customary circumstances this know-how takes many years to acquire. You've perhaps seen photos of wealthy real estate property owners. They all seem to be elderly men. However, you do not have to be advanced in years to enjoy the wealth that real estate investing may bestow. With appropriate know-how you can cut through the years and acquire "instant experience," which I feel is the key to successful investing.

You Benefit By My Experience

I did not come by my fabulous investment system by chance. I have been a builder, investor and real estate broker for over twenty-five years. During this period, I have been involved in thousands of real estate transactions. I have participated in deals involving from $500 cash to many millions. I have represented individuals buying their first parcel and sophisticated investment groups investing staggering sums of money. I was able to gain valuable experience and, in the process, learned the many secrets of successful investing. I will, throughout the pages of this book, pass this valuable information along to you. You will have in your possession the secret of making money through real estate investments.

The Magic Eleven

I have what I call my "Magic Eleven." Before purchasing an

11

investment property you must have affirmative answers to at least nine of the eleven statements listed below.

1. The income must be actual, not projected or magnified.
2. In a realty transaction the past belongs to the seller and the future to the purchaser.
3. Expenses must be adequate and complete.
4. The property should not be vulnerable to competition from a newer or larger similar property.
5. Property must be readily marketable.
6. The property should have inflationary hedges.
7. If the property has good tax advantages, this is a strong plus.
8. The property must show a fair profit.
9. Ask yourself: If the building were completely vacant, could I still achieve the same or a greater rent roll? The answer must be yes.
10. Room for expansion is a plus.
11. Cash equity should not exceed twice the gross rental.

Many of the more popular types of investment properties will be carefully analyzed through the application of the Magic Eleven. I will, by way of illustration, show typical investment listings which will then be examined so that you will learn when you should buy and when you should sell.

Anyone Can Do It

When you have completed this book, you will be able accurately to analyze investment properties. You will be able to become, even with a small amount of money, a real estate operator. You will have the opportunity to improve your financial position in a field with no ceiling whatsoever.

Financial Independence May Be Yours

My enthusiasm for this lucrative field is based upon what I have seen. I have seen salesmen, manual laborers, clerks, business people, professionals and parking lot attendants achieve wealth and financial independence. The parking lot attendant particularly comes to mind—he became a multi-millionaire.

CALVIN L. GREENBERG

Contents

1

How To Produce Riches
Through Financing

Financing has frequently been called the legs
that make an investor run. I believe that
financing is not only the legs, but also the heart
of an investor. Let us assume that a builder has
his eye on a prime office building site, with the
type of location that is adjacent to transportation. Centrally located and in an area where
there is a great shortage—and consequently a big
demand.

Carrying the assumption further, let us price
the land at $150,000. Zoning permits the erec-
tion of a 50,000 square foot building. The
location is superior, the proposed building well
laid out and the price at $3.00 per square foot is
right. Do we have a problem? Yes.

The price for the plot is $150,000. All cash. The builder has actual cash available of $50,000. This leaves him some $100,000 short. Consequently, financing is needed. Is it possible to get someone to put up part of the money needed to purchase the land? If so, who can the builder apply to for a loan? Mortgage companies specializing in short term loans will give land mortgages for a year or less.

The logical move at this juncture is for the builder to prepare plans and specifications. The plans and specifications are submitted to a permanent lender who will issue a building loan and permanent mortgage. Out of the building loan advancement the land mortgage is cleared away.

With a 50,000 square foot building, and the projected rent roll at $9.00 a square foot the gross projected rental is $450,000. All things being equal the lender would reasonably issue a commitment for four times the gross rental or $1,800,000. In many instances the lender will go along with a commitment—with reservations. The lender may require a hold back of 20% until the project is 80% leased. The "base loan advance" will be $1,440,000. Actually the builder is not terribly inconvenienced, because the $1,440,000 will cover the cost of land and building. The holdback money, $360,000, is the builder's contractor profit and entrepreneur profit. Sometimes, because of diverse circumstances, the building costs may be higher than anticipated. In reality there are periods when the builder will actually come up short. Invariably ways are found to circumvent this lack of money. The contractors will usually absorb all or most of the difference, waiting for their monies until the builder receives his final payment. Brokerage commissions may be held up until after the holdback money is available. Between the contractors and the brokers the builder can survive until his last mortgage payment.

One Job—Various Types Of Financing

Financing is very important to the survival of investment properties. In the hypothetical but typical job previously mentioned the builder required the following financial aids:

(A) Land Loan
(B) Building Loan
(C) Permanent Financing
(D) Notes to Contractor
(E) Notes to Brokers

Five separate financial aids were needed to complete the job. Without the financing aids this job would never have been built.

The innovative modes of financing are almost endless and interchangeable. In the subject job under discussion, a land mortgage could have been substituted. The builder could have worked out a land subordination mortgage with the seller of the land. This would have alleviated the money shortage for the land purchase.

Obtaining Secondary Financing

Investment in one and two family homes is sometimes difficult. The main reason for these difficulties is often an unstable mortgage market—there being periods of plentiful mortgage money and periods where money is tight. Even during the so-called normal times there may be difficulty for purchasers requiring conventional mortgages. The conventional mortgage has been the financial stepchild. V.A. and F.H.A. financing has accounted for much of the residential sales in this country. And there always seems to be a mousetrap! In one case it was superior financing. One of the more important residential builders wanted to hypo sales and actually did by working out an arrangement with a lending institution to approve 75% thirty year first mortgage financing. Then an arrangement was made with a finance company to make funds available for a 15% second mortgage. In effect the purchaser had a 90% mortgage—the secondary financing running for the same length of time as the first mortgage.

During the 1960's a new and interesting form of financing came into being, the mortgage Real Estate Investment Trusts. The Real Estate Investment Trusts serve a unique, but useful place in the world of financing. For example Jerry R., a builder, specializes in building country clubs. The clubs are built and run by Jerry, for a time—until they reach a maximum gross. A sale-leaseback is then entered into. The financing is arranged by a mortgage Real Estate Investment Trust. The financing of a country club is considered by many lending institutions to be a high risk loan. The Real Estate Investment Trusts really are not competing with banks and insurance companies in that they prefer short term building loans and other type loans that offer higher yields than conventional lending institutions are partial to. The Real Estate Investment Trusts not only prospered, but achieved the backing of banks, insurance companies and Wall Street.

People who buy and sell investment properties sometimes provide the ingredients for amusing anecdotes. I remember Hilda and Arnold, two investors. They were neither related nor married. Somehow they had gotten together and over a period of years had bought, sold, financed and retained many pieces of investment property. It was their policy to meet once a month at Hilda's house for dinner in order to discuss their properties. After a partnership of some twenty years, Hilda informed Arnold that she would like to sell all of their properties, retire and move to Florida. At this point in time the partnership owned eleven properties. Within three months they sold ten of the properties. The last remaining property proved to be an obstacle. No matter what price was offered Arnold managed to find something wrong with the deal. One prospect was an insurance company that offered to place, through a bank, a fantastic mortgage on the property, and net lease the property on a long term basis. This type of deal, while not a pure sale, still would have freed Hilda to retire to her vacation paradise. Arnold coldly rejected the offer. I made an appointment to see Arnold the next day and inquired quite bluntly why he had turned down the deal of a lifetime. Arnold explained, "It really isn't too difficult to find a good piece of real estate, but it's hard as hell to find a woman who cooks like Hilda."

An investor I know rather well is Chubby C. That's what everyone calls him. Chubby was a man of 75 years of age—who was a real estate investor. Strangely he did not become involved in real estate investing until he retired at the age of 65. Chubby's specialty was refinancing properties he purchased. I remember one deal that Chubby made—as I will point out this was typical of his operation.

Divide Realty And Prosper

Chubby bought a small medical building for $85,000 cash. The building had a $16,000 gross rental. Actually the building was worth considerably more, but the seller was unable to secure financing and consequently the building was offered free and clear. Possibly if the seller had gone to a mortgage broker he would have secured financing. Not wishing to pay a broker he wound up selling for far below the market value. Investors like Chubby quickly pounce upon deals of this type. The deal was set up as follows:

Gross Rental	$16,000
Expenses	5,000
Present Cash Flow	$11,000

Chubby formed a holding corporation to whom he sold the ground, thus separating the purchase into two separate ownerships, one for land and one for the building. Chubby then drew up a lease for ground rent in the amount of $2,500 per annum. Chubby then secured a first mortgage on the building in the amount of $64,000 at 10% interest and 1½% amortization. Not finished yet, Chubby made still another move—he mortgaged the land in the amount of $20,000 at 10% interest and 1½% amortization. The particulars now are:

Present Cash Flow	$11,000
Ground Rent Expense	2,500
1st Mortgage: $64,000 at 9%	$ 8,500
interest and 1% amortization	$ 6,400
Cash Flow	$ 2,100

The land lease was for $2,500 per annum. The $20,000 mortgage expense was $20,000, leaving a net profit on the land lease of $100. Now let's analyze Chubby's profit.

Purchase Price	$85,000
Financing	$84,000
Cash in Job	$ 1,000
Building Cash Flow	$2,100
Ground Rent	$2,500
Land Cash Flow	$ 100
Total Cash Flow	$4,700

Chubby had a total of $1,000 invested in the job and because of astute financing was earning $4,700 per annum plus amortization. Also, because of the division of land and building each could be sold separately if desired. When Chubby purchased the job his return on equity was 12.9%. After refinancing Chubby had a return on equity of 470%.

Where Can I Finance?

Some people with capital entering the world of real estate investments are wary about refinancing or financing possibilities. These anxieties are expressed in their reluctance to purchase properties with other than long term financing. This is a situation that is entirely unnecessary, because these are many sources for obtaining funds. A partial list follows:

Commercial Banks   Estate Executors
R.E.I.T. (Mortgage Trusts)   Philanthropic Organizations
Fraternal Orders   Union Funds
Mutual Savings Banks   Savings Banks
Individuals   Foundations
Individual Trustees   Charitable Institutions
Savings & Loan Associations   Corporate Trustees
Insurance Companies   Schools, Colleges, Universities
Pension Funds   Sellers (Purchase Money Financing)
                Mortgage Investment Companies

The logical question at this point is—What types of investment properties will these lending groups finance? The types of investments most easily financed are:

Various types of miscellaneous   Large shopping centers
  commercial   Net leases
Multi-family residential complexes   Parking lots and garages
Strip shopping centers and tax-   Professional centers
  payers   Industrial, individual and
Recreation properties, resorts, etc.   complexes
One and two family dwellings   Hotels and motels
Apartment buildings   Office buildings
Land   Quasi-public
Nursing homes

Loans available for these types of investment property include the following:

State and Federal Guarantees
1st and 2nd mortgages
Building improvement loans
Interim financing
Permanent loans

If any readers wish additional information regarding financing I would suggest they contact some of the following:

Mortgage Bankers Association of America
111 W. Washington Street
Chicago, Illinois 60602

Urban Renewal Administration
Lafayette Building
811 Vermont Avenue, N.W.
Washington, D.C. 20005

Small Business Administration
811 Vermont Avenue, N.W.
Washington, D.C. 20005

Farm Credit Administration
South Agriculture Building
14th Street and Independence Avenue, S.W.
Washington, D.C. 20003

National Association of Mutual Savings Banks
200 Park Avenue
New York, New York

Good Deals Are Made—Not Bought

A client of mine, Meyer G., made much money by being an operator—buying and selling investment properties. Meyer was a regular purchaser of investment properties. Five to six deals a year. Meyer could not wait around for the legendary "good deal." It was necessary for Meyer to continually buy and sell properties. Meyer achieved success through secondary financing.

A typical "Meyer" deal is one purchased in Florida. The property was a small office building with a gross rental of $20,000, expenses of $6,000, and subject to a first mortgage balance of $50,000. The cost to carry the mortgage was $6,000 per annum. A set-up revealed the following:

Gross Rental	$20,000
Estimated Expenses	6,000
Free & Clear Profit	$14,000
1st Mortgage interest & amortization	6,000
Cash Flow	$ 8,000

Purchase price $65,000 cash over the first mortgage or $115,000—to show 12.3% on equity.

Meyer turned the building over with two changes in the listing. He took back a purchase money mortgage of $40,000 at 6% interest and 2% amortization. The 6% interest rate was used in order to sweeten the deal and consequently increase the cash flow. The other change in the listing was the cash over financing, which was reduced to $48,000. Meyer walked out of the deal with $17,000, less than his original purchase. However, let us examine exactly what happened.

Original Cash Flow	$8,000
Purchase Money Mortgage Interest & Amortization	3,200
Cash Flow	$4,800

Analysis: 12% equity return to purchaser

Meyer purchased the building for $115,000 and sold the building for $138,000. A profit on the sale of $23,000. Meyer left $17,000 in the job, but in addition to his sales profit he was receiving $3,200 per annum interest and amortization on the purchase money mortgage. If we calculate a return of $3,200 on $17,000 cash the yield is 18.8%. No matter how this deal is figured Meyer winds up with a handsome profit. The moral of the story is that financing is possibly the mightiest of all real estate investment tools.

Use Qualified Realty Appraisers

I have been asked by investors how they can acquire some expert advice relative to refinancing investment properties. I believe that the very best information obtainable may be secured by employing a qualified real estate appraiser. These men are far different from the old time brokers who appraised with experienced guesses and the classic formula of so many times the gross. These estimates were very crude and of little help. How do we select a qualified real estate appraiser? An easy but worthwhile method is by employing appraisers who belong to one or more of the following societies.

> Columbia Society of Real Estate Appraisers
>
> American Institute of Real Estate Appraisers
>
> Society of Real Estate Appraisers
>
> National Association of Real Estate Appraisers

Now what makes the members of these professional societies competent real estate appraisers? The first and most important reason is education. Societies, like the Columbia Society, are educational organizations and its members are trained appraisers. The second reason is experience—which requires no explanation. The combination of training and experience is an unbeatable combination. When you can get it use it.

Tony D. was an ice man. I could give you his complete name, but you would not know of this man. Tony came to this country at the turn of the century. Tony was five years old when he arrived in this country. He came with his mother, father and two brothers. They had relatives in Astoria, Queens, New York and wound up living there. Tony grew up and attended grammar school for several years before giving up his education to go to work. He secured employment as a helper to a local ice man. The boy worked industriously and saved his money. As he grew older he went into business for himself. Tony invested much of his money in real estate. His method was to buy investments that owners though to be distressed properties. The owners thought their properties to be in trouble because their mortgages were due and they did not know where to go for refinancing or were reluctant to pay for refinancing. Tony amassed a fortune in real estate through his dealings with the scared and greedy. How did Tony secure his financing? Simple, he was astute enough to employ people who knew how to secure refinancing—mortgage brokers.

Tony did not appear to be a sophisticated investor—actually he was. Tony could barely read or write. In his own way Tony really was a sophisticated investor in that he knew a bargain when he saw one. Also, Tony was clever enough to surround himself with competent people, lawyers, mortgage brokers, real estate brokers and accountants. A wise man is one who surrounds himself with competent aides. Tony was such a man. Surrounding oneself with competent aids is surely the least expensive way to achieve financial success.

One final point, in writing this book I invariably refer to men who have had real estate experiences. I would not want to give the impression that real estate investing has no place for women, as this is not true. Possibly the best known, for her realty achievements, was the late Hetty Green. Hetty Green's specialty was financing. Buying advantageous mortgages was her business. Hetty also was famous for buying and selling investment properties—but in the Hetty Green manner. Hetty liked to buy a building and sell it for a profit—the profit being in the form of clever financing. Hetty, of course, was also famous for her frugal manner. This should not overshadow the lady's real estate accomplishments.

What To Look For

You must attempt to recognize underfinanced properties. Long term financing is beneficial, but it should be in the form of first mortgages. When the first mortgage is of the long term type, and there is no secondary financing, we have what I like to refer to as "underfinanced" property. The "underfinanced" property leaves you several interesting options.

If a property has only one mortgage and this financing is five years or less, then we have an opportunity to refinance. The refinancing should increase the mortgage, but will lower the cash equity and, in most cases, increase the yield on equity.

Another interesting option that should be taken advantage of is the purchase money mortgage. Again, it is necessary to have a property with only one mortgage. This type of option is as strong as the deal you are able to create. The seller, in order to induce a sale, will generally take back secondary financing at interest rates below the general market. This will increase your profit.

I believe that a careful study of financing possibilities must rate high on the investors' "must list." Profits may be more easily and quickly realized by watching for good financing opportunities than by following the buy low and sell high procedure.

Always watch for favorable financing. Financing has become the vehicle of progress, the conveyance that drives large businesses, countries and individuals toward their common goals—a favorable achievement.

2

The Forever Equity Formula

In commencing the writing of this book, I was faced with a difficult problem. Where to start. The logical area seemed to be money and precisely what happens to it when it is invested. The process of investing money creates two questions.

(1) What return will my investment yield?
(2) How long will it take to get back the money that I have invested?

The answer to both questions is, in truth, identical. For example, if $1,000 is invested and the return is to be 10%, then the investor will receive $100 per annum. In converse, the investor will get back his money in 10 years or 10% per annum. There are methods of changing yields via leverage, but this will be covered in a later chapter.

When purchasing investment properties you are entitled to a fair market return. Actually, fair market return is the yield on equity that each type of property will give you. Yes, each individual type property has a different yield.

Big Yield Or Little Yield?

I'm sure that you are thinking that a wise investor will, quite naturally, buy that type property which will give the investor the highest yield. Perhaps you are right. Then again, you may be wrong. The rate of return is governed by the risk. Therefore, the greater the risk, the greater the yield. Which type property should you buy? The answer is diversification. An investment portfolio should have some balance.

Balance Is A Must

Investment balance means having several different type properties with varying degrees of return. If you have all high risk properties, you will presumably make a lot of money, but chance losing it all. On the other hand, if you play it ultra safe and invest in only blue chip properties, you will have a meager yield. Consequently, balance is a must.

Know Your Investment Yields

In order to acquaint you with the normal investment yields, I have made up the chart that follows:

Illustration 2-1

TYPICAL INVESTMENT YIELDS
(return on cash equity)*

Net leases	9½%	(−1½%)	Free and clear
Office buildings	14%	(+3%)	After financing
Shopping centers	12%	(+1%)	After financing
Apartments	12%	(+1%)	After financing
Industrials	15%	(+4%)	After financing
Medical centers	12%	(+1%)	After financing

Note: *These yields are based upon a prime rate of 11%.

Taxpayers	13%	(+2%)	After financing
Land leases	10%	(−1%)	Free and clear
Gas Stations	9%	(−2%)	Free and clear
Drive-In Restaurants	10½%	(−½%)	Free and clear
Loft buildings	18%	(+7%)	After financing
Tenements	33%	(+22%)	After financing
Two family dwellings	Rent free		After financing
Leaseholds (long term)	15%	(+4%)	After financing
Sale-leasebacks	11½%	(+½%)	After financing

Prime Rate Is Your Foundation

As you read the illustration you will note that each different type of property has its own particular return. The individual return will fluctuate from time to time. However, you will be able to continue to use Illustration 2-1. The fluctuations are caused by changes in the prime rate. The illustration is based upon a prime rate of 11%. If you are not fully aware of what the prime rate is, you may call any of the large lending institutions and they will give you any information you request, including the present prime rate.

Illustration 2-1 Is Never Outmoded

Take the first property listed in Illustration 2-1, net leases, and you will note that the yield is 9½%. This rate is 1½% less than the prime rate. If the prime rate were lowered to 10%, then you could expect a yield of 8½%. You should easily be able to reach the proper yield on each different type property by adding the number in brackets to the prime rate.

You have now learned the first step in investing. You have learned how to determine what the correct market price is for each type property listed in Illustration 2-1.

Things to Remember:

(1) Money, when invested, must yield the proper return.
(2) Each different type property has its own particular yield.
(3) Investment portfolios, if possible, should be diversified.
(4) The prime rate is your foundation for determining fair market prices.

(516) 746-2555-6

(212) 423-6376

BALTER & GREENBERG, INC.

"The Nations Prestige Realty Firm"
182 Hillside Avenue, Williston Park, New York 11596

CALVIN L. GREENBERG
Chairman of the Board

JACK BALTER
President

LEE WEISINGER
Vice Pres., Investments

SOLOMON GOODMAN
Vice Pres., Leasing

IF INTERESTED PLEASE RETURN
THIS FORM IN ENCLOSED POSTAGE-
FREE ENVELOPE

THIS INFORMATION STRICTLY CONFIDENTIAL

CHECK IF	TYPE OF	MINIMUM
INTERESTED	PROPERTY	REQUIRED RETURN

1. ( ) SINGLE TENANT NET DEALS, AAA-1 TENANT   (%)
   ( ) NEIGHBORHOOD TAXPAYERS   (%)
   ( ) SHOPPING CENTERS   (%)
   ( ) OFFICE BUILDINGS   (%)

2. ARE YOU INTERESTED IN <u>LOCAL,</u> <u>OUT OF TOWN</u> OR <u>BOTH?</u>
          (CIRCLE ONE)

3. MAXIMUM CASH AVAILABLE FOR ONE DEAL $_____
          (WRITE AMOUNT)

4. DO YOU HAVE ANY OF THE FOLLOWING FOR SALE?
          (CHECK, IF FOR SALE)

                    TAXPAYER   _____

                    OFFICE BLDG.   _____

                    SHOPPING CENTER   _____

                    NET DEAL   _____

                    INTERESTED IN A TRADE?   _____

5. ARE YOU PRINCIPAL, BROKER (CIRCLE ONE)

Remarks:
<u>NAME</u>:

<u>ADDRESS</u>:   <u>TELEPHONE</u>:

6. I AM NO LONGER INTERESTED ( ) CHECK

Illustration 2-2

What To Look For

On every occasion use the "Forever Equity Formula" in order to determine what the correct yield should be for the class of property concerned. If the yield is too great, try to determine why. Verify expenses to ascertain if they are accurate. One of the most flagrant abuses is the omission of amortization from the expenses. Also, pay no attention to amortization being added to the cash flow in order to create a generous but non-existent profit. This type of trickery only creates paper profits.

In describing what to look for it is most important, I believe, to stress what *not* to look for. Don't look for fantastic bargains—you will get yourself into trouble. Your goal should be the typical investment yield for the type of property you are interested in acquiring. In your search for properties you will be communicating with brokers concerning their offerings. The brokers will, from time to time, send you questionnaires (See Illustration 2-2). These inquiries should be answered correctly. If you understate your yield the broker will assume that you are "low balling" him. If you write down an extremely high yield, the broker will decide that you are impossible and will throw away your name. Be honest with your broker—it will pay dividends.

3

Getting The Highest Return On Your Investment

The basic formula for the real estate investor should be to achieve the greatest possible return—with safety. If this reads like an enigma I suppose it is. Investors should seek the return of their capital—at 20%, at 12% or 7%. Actually all returns on equity are correct for different investors. Each investor must decide upon the investment category into which he falls.

The investor who seeks 12% on equity generally falls into the category of average investor. "The average investor" is an inadequate term and actually should read—the majority of investors. Within this bracket is contained that group having $75,000 to $150,000 cash for investment in a single transaction. Within this price range the investor may purchase a small apartment building, taxpayer, or strip center. Net leases and sale leasebacks are, as a general rule, priced out of this category. (I will discuss in another part of this book yields on equity variances.) However, assuming that a mean yield is 12%, then this is the rate at which the investor is achieving the highest return on his investment. Don't look for 13%-14% or accept 11%. Not unless you can carefully explain to yourself why you are getting more or taking less. Don't fool yourself into believing that sellers are unaware of market yields. Any seller may easily learn of market prices through any of the following:

1. Discussing their property with investment brokers.
2. Having a professional appraisal made.
3. Searching municipal records for comparative sales of similar properties in the area.

Be Wary Of "Bargains"

Having established that sellers are pretty much up on market values, we should consider why 12% properties are sometimes offered for sale at 15% to 18% yields. An interesting bargain was offered to me several years ago. The property was a well built garden apartment. I carefully checked the listing and found the expense figures to be pretty reasonable. The insurance, water, sewer, electric, repairs, help and vacancy factors appeared to be accurate. The financing was heavy and the taxes were quite low. Return on equity was 15%, comparable properties yielded 12%.

I began to do some investigating. The mortgage was high, even though self-liquidating it might possibly present a big problem. I then checked comparable garden apartments in the area and found that their taxes were 33% of gross income. The subject property was only taxed at 10% of gross income. Further investigation revealed that the owner had misrepresented. The amount on the tax bill would have been the amount that he previously stated. How then did the owner misrepresent? Well, he used an old trick—partial assessment. Keen builders will attempt to get their certificate of occupancy after the last date for assessing properties. Those properties assessed after the last date of assessment receive a partial assessment. The next year the property is fully assessed. In this manner the builder can achieve a larger first year profit and offset start up losses.

The particular property offered to me showed 15%, a full 3%

above the market value for such properties. However, when fully assessed, the taxes would be increased, approximately 23% of gross. This would have wiped out the entire profit. Suddenly my bargain property became a full fledged lemon. The big problem with the property was the top heavy mortgage that ate up too much of the profits. In effect the builder sold his property when he received his mortgage. Investigate bargains carefully as they may be booby trapped.

Big Return Equals Big Risk

Another group of investors is the 20% group. Basically this group is composed of investors in the $15,000 to $30,000 category. The credo of a great many of this group appears to be "20% or bust." More often than not they have a fine chance of going busted. The fact that these people invest less money does not mean that they are entitled to greater profits. In this group are many inexperienced investors who mistakenly believe that real estate investing is a sure path to riches. This may be true, but not without either experience or a reasonable amount of knowledge—either acquired or purchased.

An example of what I mean is best expressed in the following tale. A friend asked me to take a look at a supposedly advantageous property that he had just purchased. The property contained three stores—all vacant. It seemed that this taxpayer had had a bad fire. The old tenants did not choose to move back into the building. The landlord subsequently settled with the insurance company and rebuilt the building. The property was purchased to show a hypothetical 20% yield on equity. To actually achieve this yield the three stores would have to be rented for $250 per month each. I inspected the property and advised my friend that he should have no trouble renting the stores for $250 per month. Knowing my friend to be a do-it-yourself advocate I strongly suggested that he employ a commercial leasing broker to handle the leasing and a real estate lawyer to handle the drawing of the leases. My friend laughingly informed me that he was going to save the expense of brokers and lawyers. I wished him luck.

A man of his word, my friend leased the three stores by himself and also drew up his own leases. The three stores were leased to a luncheonette, launderette and beauty parlor. The first mistake was in leasing to three tenants who all used a considerable amount of water, so much so that the cesspools subsequently overflowed. There was nothing that could be done—the cesspools could not take all of the water. The plot was not large enough to build larger cesspools. The water overflowed, the town issued summonses and the tenants sued. This was only the beginning. The leases did not contain tax stops. Too bad. The taxpayer was completely rebuilt after the fire and because it was practically a new building the municipal authorities hit the property with a whopping assessment. Within the next three years the local tax rate increased substantially. The net result was to wipe out most of the profit that the building showed on paper. Problems seemed unending for this property. Both the luncheonette and the beauty parlor were considered bad fire risks and the insurance company set a high fire rate on the building. A real estate lawyer would have protected the owner against any large increases in taxes and fire insurance—there was no lawyer and consequently no protection.

My friend owned a building that was costing him $50 per week for pumping cesspools, had very high taxes and high insurance rates. Back to my original premise, getting the highest return on your investment. This can only be done by selecting a property you like and then conferring with your lawyer, accountant and real estate broker. Use experts for maximum safety.

Professional Advice Prevents Problems

I am not attempting to give the impression that investment properties are difficult to operate. They are not. The situations mentioned in this chapter thus far have been fraught with problems. A careful analysis reveals that the problems are not management problems, but rather inherited problems—problems that could have been prevented prior to purchase. The highest possible return for an investment property may be achieved by careful scrutiny of financing and all expense items. Don't become hungry when the cash flow appears exceptionally generous.

Another sale that comes to mind is the purchase of a medical building by a Dr. Stock. Dr. Stock assumed that being a medical man made him a natural to buy a medical building. So, Dr. Stock, without consulting anyone, and despite his knowing absolutely nothing about real estate, purchased a medical building. The property was supposed to yield 10% after interest and amortization payments. The actual cash flow proposed was $20,000 per annum. The doctor's cash investment was $200,000—a tidy sum.

The doctor operated the building for one year and then learned that his cash flow was only $10,000 or 5% on equity. He did not have any vacancies and his expenses were approximately as represented. What happened to the lost $10,000? Actually nothing happened to the $10,000—it never really was there. The doctor read a listing, did not understand what he read, but insisted to his attorney that he was completely aware of all factors concerning the property. What actually happened was that the doctor, when checking the rent roll, saw the letters AV after each tenant's name. The AV was the average rental, much higher than the present rental. Actually the doctor didn't make out too badly—the financing had heavy amortization and ten years later the doctor refinanced and recaptured a substantial sum. The doctor's problems could have been prevented had he listened to his attorney at the time of contract. I'm always curious why some men pay goodly sums for advice and then refuse to take the very advice that they have purchased. A sad waste of money.

Give A Little—Make A Lot

An interesting situation I recall occurred in the state of Washington. A well known investor negotiated for the purchase of a seven-store taxpayer. If successful in purchasing the property, the operator planned to advise all the tenants whose leases were up for renewal that their leases would not be renewed. The operator had concluded a lease subject to his purchasing this property with a junior department store. The operator insisted upon possession in order to completely renovate the building to suit his new tenant.

The building was owned by two elderly maiden ladies. The two little old ladies operated a launderette in the building—their greatest pleasure being in watching the shoppers pass by in front of their store. When the operator mentioned his plan for the property the two ladies declined to sell. At that time there wasn't sufficient money in the world that would get them to surrender their front seats on main street. The operator stood to suffer the loss of an admirable deal. The broker tried to persuade the old ladies but was unsuccessful. The operator's lawyer tried to convince the two elderly ladies and he also failed. The deal seemed doomed.

The operator decided that now was the time to talk with the ladies himself. He made a plea to the ladies and also failed. Then he had an idea. Why not duplicate the situation that the old ladies loved? The operator secured an option on a launderette located three blocks away. The launderette was offered to the ladies at cost. The ladies showed interest, but hemmed and hawed at the price. Eventually the deal was closed—at a drop in price of $5,000. Giving the old ladies their ringside seat had cost the operator $5,000 out of his own pocket.

The operator had figured to induce a profit of $105,000 on the entire transaction, instead he had made $100,000. I don't think the operator's profit was inadequate. If a man can make ten deals like this he becomes a millionaire.

This particular transaction has shown that in order to obtain the highest return on your investment it is sometimes necessary to give a little and not lose the deal. Also, a little skillful contrivance sometimes is a great aid.

In this, our most sophisticated world, we still have superstition. Believe it or not some people purchase investment properties based, not upon return or other legitimate factors, but upon lucky days and jinxs.

Buy Facts—Not Emotions

A woman inherited an apartment building upon the death of her husband. The lady's husband had been killed in an automobile accident. The man was past seventy years of age. The woman was elderly and not able to manage the property herself so she hired her nephew to manage the building. The nephew was disposed to drink, and one day while "loaded" he ran his car off an embankment and was killed. One week later the distraught widow, completely shaken, was going to the building via taxicab. The cab tangled with a bus and the widow was severely hurt. The score was now three auto accidents to three people—all going to a particular apartment building. The woman decided to sell the building. There were no takers. People had decided that the building was jinxed. Everyone seemed to have heard about the building and just to be on the safe side they decided to avoid this property. This seemed absolutely crazy. This was the United States where voodoo, witch doctors, superstition and curses are supposed to be non-existent. Yet here was a building supposedly out to kill or maim its owner. In order to try to attract a buyer the price was lowered. There were no takers. Determined to unshackle herself from the jinxed building the widow again lowered the price. This time a smart operator snapped up the building. The sale of the building occurred some fifteen years ago. The building was held by the operator for one year and then resold. I am happy to report that both the operator and his purchaser are both alive and in good health. The series of accidents that happened were pure coincidence. In this instance the operator was able to get the highest return on his investment by taking advantage of a unique situation.

In order to secure the most for your investment you must keep a cool head and never lose sight of the terms of the deal that you are trying to achieve.

Sellers use all means of human emotion in order to turn an advantage. The many emotions you may run into during a contract are not limited to, but will include at various times, moral weakness, greed, deceit, humor, and subterfuge, not to mention all types of dialogue. Do not deviate from the original deal and you will eliminate most problems.

In order to have a proper idea of the existing investment market and to have ample exposure to the properties being offered for sale it is necessary to look at about 10-12 properties per week. For the majority of investors it is not possible to spare the time necessary to look at that many properties. Most investors fall into two categories, retired people and those who are in a business other than real estate. The former group does not wish to spend full time searching for investments while the latter group does not have the necessary time.

For The Busy Man—Syndication

For those investors lacking the time to seek investments there are those who can be of great service—syndicators. I do not refer to the type of syndicators who were popular during the early sixties. These syndicators sponsored huge public offerings that had hundreds of investors in each deal. Far different is today's syndicator. Generally there are from 5-20 limited partners with the syndicator being the general partner. Yields are about two points below the general market, but in my opinion well worth the two point cost. The syndicator of today is usually an experienced real estate man whose only occupation is in the seeking, buying, syndicating and operation of investment properties. It is the syndicator to whom investors without too much time for their investments should turn. After the initial investment the investor receives periodic reports and dividend checks. For the busy or retired investor this is a marvelous way of getting the highest return on an investment.

Different Types Of Syndications

Throughout the fifties the small investors were frantically acquiring syndications. Shares were sold for as little as $500 each. With all of this money about, the wheeler-dealers quickly leaped in to establish their share of this money. Unfortunately a great number of these people had little or no experience. Money was made and money was lost. A great quantity of the money that was lost was lost because of inexperienced syndicators and lack of government restraint. Because of these conditions syndication became slightly disreputable.

Syndication, prior to the explosion of the fifties, made its debut in this country in Boston, Massachusetts about one hundred years ago. At that particular time it was illegal for a corporation to own real estate for investment purposes. The only real estate that a corporation might own was real estate used exclusively for its own business. To be more specific, a corporation could only own real estate that it used for its offices, plant buildings, and the land under these properties. In order to circumvent this law the Boston Real Estate Investment Trust was formed. Small investors were welcome and they invested in much the same manner that one invests in Wall Street stocks. During the 30's another innovation reached its peak in the form of mortgage bonds. Little investors were able to purchase small portions of large mortgages. The 30's was deep within the depths of the great depression and there were many failures, including mortgage bonds.

In 1961, syndication assumed a new role. Real Estate Investment Trusts were granted special tax advantages provided that they conformed to certain regulations. The Treasury department was placed in charge of seeing that these regulations were adhered to. Basically, these rules are as follows:

    (a) 90% of the net income must be paid out to investors.

    (b) There must be 100 or more stockholders.

    (c) Not more than 50% may be owned by five or more persons.

    (d) 75% of the gross income must come from real estate related investments.

The Real Estate Investment Trusts have done well and the small investors have found a place to put their money with reasonable safety and many tax advantages.

There are many ways for an investor to secure the highest yield on syndication investment. It is, however, the investor's obligation to select the particular syndication method that most easily fits in with his own investment ambitions. The investor must pick the mode most applicable to himself and adhere to the system until conditions dictate adopting a new one.

How Not To Get Big Returns

There is an investment difficulty that needs consideration—both from neophyte and skillful investors. I submit the phenomenon known popularly as "the boom." The boom is exceedingly like a ball that is cast up into the atmosphere relying upon the impetus used. The ball travels upward and upward until it is spent—then it quickly plummets to earth. The investment boom is to a degree not different—every time terminating in a quiet annihilation of its power.

At the time a boom inflicts itself it is propelled with the fury of a sickening disease. A boom parcel of real estate may be dealt as frequently as ten times. Down to earth people unexpectedly grow to be immediate speculators. Prices zoom out of vision. Only more suddenly the boom bursts. Most of the speculators discover themselves wiped out and the property reverts to whomever holds the first mortgage. From time to time there has been conversation about government intervention in order to prevent such a happening. This is not a practical solution, but there is a solution. Real estate investment brokers should attempt to advise clients when they see a boom on the rise. Further, the clients must seek out established brokerage firms—firms that are familiar with and have previously seen the result of booms.

During a boom a great many investors are stricken with a mania to buy, regardless of price. During the height of a boom the frenzy, the wild enthusiasm is beyond belief. Real estate brokers are in their offices for days on end; offices littered with old, stale coffee cups, sandwich wrappers on the floor and hectic bidding by over-anxious investors. There is no regard for any of the aspects of intelligent buying or selling. Properties continually change hands sight unseen. Investors forget everything they know and purchase real estate for one reason alone—because the property is in the boom area.

The overzealous investor has an additional problem—the "go-go broker." During periods when a boom is taking place, new brokerage firms pop up like mushrooms. These brokers are interested in selling anything that they can. There is no regard for safety or intelligent investing. Reputable brokers do not like boom periods. When the bubble has burst investors are very cautious and most reluctant to invest in anything. The go-go brokers disappear after the boom recedes, but they leave problems for the remaining legitimate brokers.

In striving to achieve the greatest return on your investment follow conventional channels. Do not seek out short cuts; more often than not they will spell failure.

What To Look For

It is important that you purchase the type property that best fits your needs. These needs should be met in three ways.

(1) Type of property
(2) Adequate return on equity
(3) Opportunity to increase yield

Every investor is entitled to acquire the highest possible yield that may be gotten. In order to accomplish this he must not hope to find the "big yield" floating about, waiting for a prospective purchaser to snap it up. To achieve the "big yield" you must look for a property that lends itself to improvement of the cash flow through the methods outlined in this chapter. Also, do not purchase a property because you like its looks. Pride of ownership is pleasant, but only if it has a proper cash flow.

It is important to look for comparables when buying an investment property. If you are offered a property that you are interested in purchasing you should go to a local city hall and check. deeds for recent deals of similar properties. Checking the recent sales records is the best way to establish true market value—all things being equal.

Look for proper return on equity, because if an emergency occurs and you must sell, your property will be liquid. Real estate investment properties have historically had an active market when offered at market value.

While it is true that great fortunes have sometimes been made through a single investment it is also possible to be wiped out in a single investment if you are greedy. I suggest that you look for areas that are having booms. Then avoid these areas. *Boom properties are high risk and must be avoided.*

4

How To Use Depreciation To Your Greatest Advantage

Depreciation, or tax shelter as it is also referred to, is a unique gift to the real estate industry by the government. I say unique because it has been denied to savings and stocks and bonds. The government has determined that an investment property's net profit, for taxation purposes, may pay taxes less a proportional distribution of the decrease in value due to wear.

The depreciation allowance covers the partial cost of most real estate properties. Real estate like all other manufactured commodities has a limited economic life. Based upon the length of economic value, the government has developed a depreciation schedule. The depreciation applies to the improvement, but not to the land underneath the improvement. The governmental determination is that land never wears out and consequently cannot be depreciated. The depreciation allowance does not apply to an individual's residence or to properties held for resale such as a builder's inventory.

The governmental theory of depreciation does not take into account the possibility of economic value change. Depreciation and estimate of worth would seem to receive small consideration. Also, only original cost and not replacement value may be recoverable.

Purchasing a property because it has great tax shelter may be a serious mistake. In addition to tax benefits a property must make sense as a real estate investment. In fact it should make sense as a real estate investment *first*.

Tax Shelter—Two Types

There are two types of shelter that we as real estate people are concerned with. One is limited and the other is splashover. The limited shelter is sufficient only to shelter taxable income from one property. The splashover shelter will shelter additional incomes.

In order to demonstrate where there is an indication of good real estate, then good depreciation, I will illustrate a property recently represented for sale.

Listing of Property For Sale

Location:	Los Angeles, California
Size:	300' x 150' (45,000 square feet)
Description:	6 story elevator apartment building containing a total of 48 apartments plus a tenant parking area. Forty-year-old building.
Assessed Value:	Land $15,000. Total $190,000.
1st Mortgage:	$450,000—Savings Bank—10 years. 8% interest and 1% amortization.

Income:		
Rents		$143,000
Parking		5,700
Washing Machines		1,300
Total		$150,000

Expenses:		
Interest & amortization	$40,500	
Real Estate Taxes	51,096	

	Water/Sewer	2,000	
	Salary	5,000	
	Heat	6,000	
	Gas & Electric	2,000	
	Elevator Maintenance	2,000	
	Repairs, maintenance	8,600	
	Insurance	3,800	$120,996
			$ 29,004

P.M. 2nd Mortgage:	$100,000 at 8% interest, 1% amortization, 10 years	9,000
Cash Flow:		$ 20,004

Price:	$200,000 cash over financing	
Depreciation Picture	Cash Flow	$20,000
	Amortization 1st mortgage	4,500
	Amortization 2nd mortgage	1,000
	Profit	$25,500
	4% tax depreciation, straight line	25,500
		Tax Free

Note: Ratio of land to building is $15,000: $175,000 or 8½% land and 91.5% building. (Land $112,500—building $637,500). Because of building's age 4% straight line depreciation used. 4% of $637,500 equals $25,000.

The listing previously demonstrated is a proper example of beneficial real estate. It's a well-located apartment building showing a reasonable cash flow, plus good financing. The depreciation, while excellent, should come second. However, where the combination of good property and sufficient tax shelter is available, my suggestion is to buy, before someone else beats you to it.

Tax shelter is of prime importance in that it is a considerable money saver. Purchasers, especially those with high incomes, are naturally quite concerned with sheltering their income. Sometimes in their anxiety to achieve shelter they purchase inadequate properties.

There are some operators who prey upon these investors who are eagerly seeking tax shelter. Quality tenancy is offered at outlandish prices. A prime example is the following listing which was recently offered for sale.

Location:	Maine	
Tenancy:	AAA-1 tenant—$500,000 net worth.	
Price:		$200,000
1st Mortgage:	$150,000 Savings Bank, due 22 years, 8½% interest and 1½% amortization. Constant.	$150,000
Cash Required		50,000
Lease:	20 years with parent company guarantee. Fully net. All expenses paid by tenant.	
Rental:	(Net net net)	$ 15,000
Expenses:	Interest and amortization	15,000
Cash Flow:		(zero)
	Amortization	$ 1,875
	Profit	$ 1,875

Tax Shelter:	Total Price	$200,000	
	Land Cost	20,000	
	Building	$180,000	
Analysis:	Profit		($ 1,875)
	4% straight line depreciation		7,200
	Tax Shelter		$ 5,325

The above listing is a trap for the unwary. The prospect is told that he is paying off a mortgage plus having a tax free income. While these statements are true, they still do not make this property a reasonable one to purchase.

1st: There is no cash flow.

2nd: All properties have mortgages, except some quality, AAA-1 net leases. However, these properties will generally have a competitive cash flow.

3rd: It is not unusual to be able to purchase properties with moderate tax shelter. A plus is the fact that all investment properties may take a depreciation allowance.

4th: The financing is based upon AAA-1 tenancy. If the tenant fails to renew his lease it will not be possible to refinance with a like mortgage. Even with a AAA-1 tenancy it is still doubtful if such refinancing could be secured. The existing financing is obviously a sweetheart mortgage.

Four Methods of Depreciation

There are four general methods of depreciation and all afford a distinctive kind of tax shelter, each being somewhat different.

The least elaborate type of depreciation is straight line. In this kind of depreciation only the improvement is depreciated according to a factor found in the I.R.S. schedule of useful life. In investment properties the depreciation factor ranges from 4% down to 1.6%. Straight line is the type of depreciation used to the greatest degree.

Another type of depreciation is the 150% declining balance method. This method is available only to the first owner or user. The factor is arrived at in the same manner as the straight line depreciation, the difference being that the depreciation is 50% greater and is taken each year on a declining balance.

A third method used is the sum-of-the-years-digits method. This method is easier to explain by example. Suppose a property has a thirty-year life. We then add up the numbers from one to thirty which gives us 465. The depreciation works as follows:

$$\text{Basis for depreciation:} \qquad \$50,000$$

$$\$50,000 \text{ times } \frac{30}{465} = \$3,225 \text{ 1st year}$$

$$\$50,000 \text{ times } \frac{29}{465} = \$3,118 \text{ 2nd year}$$

etc. for a period of thirty years.

The fourth method is easy to explain, but a little more difficult to carry out. This method is known as the composite depreciation method. The building is broken down into component parts—masonry, plumbing, carpentry, etc. It is used with new buildings as a rule.

Since 1969, when real estate tax laws were substantially reformed, residential rental property has been favored over other types of real estate. The first user of residential rental property has been permitted to use the double-declining-balance method. This is a method wherein the first user may take double ordinary, or straight line depreciation, on a declining basis. For a number of years this method provides maximum tax shelter.

Who is the first user? Who is the second user? Position of user may sometimes be difficult to prove. Methods used are the following:

1. Date of lease of earliest tenant.
2. When tenant took possession.
3. Issuance of a C.O.
4. Closing of permanent financing.
5. Who accepts first rent?

The Internal Revenue Service does not clearly define its position. Consequently, care should be taken to substantiate a first user claim. Depreciation is a tremendous plus for real estate. The Wall Street "experts" tell us that real estate has two main drawbacks—

1. Lack of liquidity.
2. Long term financing required.

Because of these "drawbacks" they claim that laws governing depreciation favor real estate in order to give real estate a much-needed break. This myth is believed by many, the conviction being based, probably, on the age-old belief that if a lie is told often enough it will in time be believed.

Real estate, like stocks, has an instant sales price. Any competent broker can advise an investor almost to the penny as to a selling price. Now, selling a security will take, from time of sell order to actual receipt of money, about eight days. A real estate contract of sale can be arranged in less time. The vast majority of securities have no tax shelter. All real estate has depreciation—or sheltered income.

The second item, long term financing, is a plus rather than a liability. Financing enlarges the investment climate and creates new outlets. There is no danger of an investor losing his property if real estate prices dip. However, when securities drop the margin calls create sudden misfortune. I might also add that a great many real estate transactions are, today, made on a free and clear basis. The scope of these transactions is in the net lease field.

To summarize, the investment product has all the benefits of securities plus the government-given privilege of depreciation—an advantage over most security investments.

What To Look For

If your financial bracket is such that a tax shelter is of prime importance then you are bound to direct your attention to tax advantages. An oversimplification is looking for large buildings on small plots. Another oversimplification is to obtain buildings built on low priced land. Both concepts are sound, but with important exceptions.

Big buildings on small plots may prove to be excellent tax shelter vehicles, but many properties fitting this description are old, and risky financial ventures. The paper tax loss, anticipated, may turn into a very real, actual cash loss. It is important to carefully look into the prospects of a reasonable cash flow. If the investment appears potentially advantageous then the tax aspects should be considered, but only as a secondary issue.

Another readily adopted concept concerns the building of new buildings on low priced land. Again we have a nice paper profit showing good tax shelter. However, the important question should be the availability of profit to shelter. It is reasonable to assume that if the land price is quite low, then the location warrants this price. In other words, we are probably dealing with a weak location. A weak location will breed weak tenancy and subsequently a weak investment. Tax shelter is important, but should not be the sole reason for making a purchase. Look out for sellers who make up beautiful set-ups allegedly showing their properties to be 100% tax free. These "sharpies" work backwards in order to achieve "tax free" properties. If the proper yearly depreciation is 3%, these people create set-ups using, say, 5%. The extra 2% may make the property appear, incorrectly, to be tax free. This type of deceptive salesmanship can easily be checked. The Internal Revenue Service has a bulletin available that outlines the yearly allowable depreciation rates. Apply these rates in order to determine proper depreciation.

5

How To Obtain Financing Through Wrap-Arounds

The Wrap-Around Mortgage

In most professions, trades, businesses, etc. there appears to be a criterion for expertise. Knowledge of any one particular phase of an industry may earmark a man as an expert in all other phases. Real estate shows little difference from other industries in that we also respect what we have little or no knowledge of. I refer to the mysterious phrase *wrap-around mortgage.*

In truth, the wrap-around mortgage appears to be an unknown quantity to the vast majority of real estate investors. The gut feeling appears to be that a working knowledge of wrap-around mortgage financing makes one a sophisticated investor. Actually this is truth. The wrap-around is a unique type of financing in that it may be used in different ways to fulfill different individual requirements. This mortgage marvel goes above and beyond any other type of financing. This mode of mortgage financing has the capability to make poor deals good and good deals better. A new baby in the world of financing within the United States, the wrap-around technique has only been in use for the past decade. However, other nations have used this technique for many years.

When Is The Wrap-Around Used?

The fundamental operation is to bring to a more desirable condition an investment transaction by affording financial leverage. There are definite situations that particularly lend themselves to the wrap-around, or blanket mortgage as it is sometimes called. The wrap-around is particularly effective during periods of high interest rates.

When an owner has a first mortgage, at an interest rate that is lower than the existing rate, and he requires additional funds, he may contact his lending institution. The probability is that his loan may be a number of years old, when rates were lower and his application now will be rejected. Even a request to raise the mortgage back to its original amount will be rejected. If the lending institution can lend money at higher rates it will assuredly seize advantage of this situation. Lofty interest rates will penetrate into the cash flow and so the property owner looks elsewhere.

Basically, most lending institutions charge within the same rate range. The only other access open would appear to be secondary financing. However, secondary financing is going from bad to worse for the reason that secondary financing, by its very nature, is far more expensive than first mortgage financing. We now have the ideal situation for a wrap-around mortgage.

Another situation ideally suited for the wrap-around appears when an owner has a first mortgage with either no prepayment privilege or an excessive prepayment penalty, secondary financing of course, being too expensive. Again the opportunity for a wrap-around.

What Is A Wrap-Around?

The wrap-around is actually a second mortgage. The wrap-around is fully subordinated to the existing first mortgage. The face value of the wrap-around mortgage is the amount of the total of the first and second mortgages. Upon receiving the total interest and amortization payment, the mortgagee of the wrap-around mortgage makes the first mortgage payment.

The interest rate of the wrap-around is generally about equal to existing first mortgage interest rates. The interest and amortization rate, paid by the mortgagor, is computed upon the face amount of the wrap-around mortgage.

How The Wrap-Around Works

To be more explicit let me cite an example. A client had a garage type property with a $100,000 balance on his first mortgage. He had just secured a new tenant for his property. The tenant was a strong AAA-1 firm whose occupancy would greatly enhance the value of the property. However, in order to make the deal a $30,000 alteration was necessary. The landlord had to somehow raise $30,000.

A first mortgage was not a possibility, because of an excessive prepayment penalty. A second mortgage was also a problem. With bonuses, second mortgages were costing approximately 18%. The only solution was a wrap-around mortgage.

A wrap-around was secured and the mathematics was as follows:

Wrap-Around:

$130,000 @ 8% interest—2% amortization.

Note: This includes $100,000 balance on first mortgage plus $30,000 additional funds.

Yearly payment $13,000

Existing 1st Mortgage:

$100,000 @ 6% interest—2% amortization.

Original amount $110,000 yearly payment	$ 8,800
Addition Payment	$ 4,200

Why does the mortgagee give a wrap-around mortgage? In this case the mortgagee incentive was provided by the $4,200 payment on a $30,000 loan. With 2%, or $600 going toward amortization, and the balance of $3,600 going toward interest—the lender has a yield of 12%.

On the other hand the property owner was only paying 8% interest and 2% amortization for the total amount of the loan, this rate of interest being the present rate, at this time, for first mortgage financing.

Other Wrap-Around Features

Prepayment on wrap-around is very limited. Payment is sometimes prohibited or at best, permitted after the 15th year. The mortgagee will insist upon these terms in order to make the transaction more attractive. In general the right to prepay any or all of the first mortgage is prohibited. There is no form wrap-around as each mortgage is tailored for a particular situation.

The terms of the wrap-around include terms identical with the first mortgage, with the exception of the interest, amortization and generally the mortgage balance, and those terms peculiar to the structure of the wrap-around.

After the wrap-around is placed, the property owner no longer makes his first mortgage payments, the total payment being made to the wrap-around mortgagee.

The wrap-around is a unique financing devise. Its most important feature is its pliability and its ability to help in the creation of deals. The wrap-around is actually a super purchase money mortgage. A mortgage that may make a difference of 1-2 points in equity yields. This can be the difference in making or losing a deal.

Also benefited by the elasticity of the wrap-around are the property owners who are not interested in selling, but who have other problems. I refer to the following situations:

(1) Mortgages that cannot be prepaid.
(2) Mortgages with very high prepayment penalties.
(3) Owners wishing to increase mortgage balances.
(4) Those owners with unfavorable mortgage terms seeking relief.

A summation of the wrap-around creates a most favorable picture—one of a mortgage that can help everyone. It helps real estate buyers, real estate sellers, and those who wish to hold their properties. The wrap-around may in time prove itself to be the strongest weapon in the financing arsenal of the realty industry.

What To Look For

The wrap-around mortgage may aid the purchase of a deal that might otherwise be difficult to acquire. Consequently the acquisition of this type of financing is important. Where do you look for it? The best source I have found is the Real Estate Investment Trusts. Generally these firms are able to underwrite the financing needed to create the wrap-around. A particularly choice opportunity is to receive an offering from one of the R.E.I.T.'s. Under these conditions I would suggest you negotiate for a wrap-around.

The existence of the wrap-around has been a boon to investors, but certain guidelines must necessarily be observed. New buildings do not lend themselves to the wrap-around. The ideal property to look for is a 15 year old building with a similarly aged mortgage, little or no prepayment penalty and an interest rate at about three points below the existing new mortgage rate.

If the purchaser is negotiating for a property that already has a wrap-around it is mandatory that he look over the mortgage terms. It is mandatory that he carefully check for the prepayment clause. Some wrap-arounds can be prepaid, but most cannot. Look for properties that have upgraded their tenancies, but not their financing. With additional tenant security a really advantageous wrap-around may be secured.

For the investor who already owns a good parcel of investment property there is also something to look for. Suppose this investor needs cash. If his property conforms to the wrap-around format then the owner may be able to secure the cash he requires and to also retain ownership of his property.

6

When To Buy Or Sell: The Key To High Profits

At what time to buy or sell a property may be a most difficult situation for buyer and seller. Possibly the most basic emotion to be dealt with is greed. The tendency for some buyers is to assume that they, and they alone, are the only available purchaser. This attitude is genuinely tragic, because this class of buyer is actually a bird-dog who flushes out a good price for someone else.

A different type of buyer is the one who is sometimes referred to as the "50 per center," so called because of his tendency to always offer 50 per cent of the asking equity cash. The old 50 per center will never buy anything, but his enjoyment is in pointing out properties to friends and saying, "I could have bought that property." To me these are sad words.

Sellers, of course, have their own peculiarities. There is the once a year seller who offers his property for sale about once every year. When he receives a solid offer the property is promptly withdrawn. Is he crazy? No, not at all. This seller is curious about the yearly value of his property. What better way to learn true value than to receive a bonafide offer. This is in effect a free appraisal. Actually I could go on and on with the various types of sellers. However, let me describe some of them in greater detail.

Greed The Profit Killer

I have a friend, Nathan L., a real estate broker. Nathan consummated a transaction and instead of a cash commission he consented to accept a 150' x 100' parcel in New Jersey. The parcel was improved with a big barn that was of little value. The parcel had been taken in lieu of a $15,000 commission.

Immediately upon taking title, he put up the property for sale. Six months passed by, then a year, and not a single offer. Nathan tried signs, newspaper advertising, other brokers—all to no avail. It appeared as though no one desired the parcel. On top of all this, taxes and assessments came to $850 for the first year. In addition the neighborhood had peaked out and was on the downgrade. What had seemed a fantastic opportunity was now beginning to appear a little sour.

Just when things looked their worst Nathan received a communication from a major oil company inquiring if the property was available. An appointment was arranged at Nathan's home. On the appointed day, with Nathan and his wife present, the oil company representative made a very interesting proposition. Nathan was offered $5,000 per annum net net net. The company proposed, at its own expense, to erect a gas station. Adopting the attitude of "don't let the man out of the room," Nathan accepted on the basis of a long term lease, at the proposed price. A lease was to be drawn and sent to the company. Instead of a lease being drawn Nathan contacted the company and requested another meeting. At this meeting, his wife, who had now taken over, insisted that the price for the land lease be increased to $6,000. The representative for the oil company promised to convey the new price request to his superior. After about ten days Nathan was advised that the oil company would meet his price. Again Nathan's wife introduced herself into the negotiations and advised the oil company that she had changed her mind and that the price was now $7,000. As he had before, the oil company representative advised Nathan's wife that he would contact his superior.

Several months later Nathan and his "negotiating wife" began to realize that perhaps they had overstated the property's value. The oil company was contacted and they politely responded with the information that they had signed a lease for another property. Eventually, after paying taxes year after year, Nathan dropped the property for non-payment of taxes.

When you have real estate to sell, arrive at a price you desire. You must, however, remember that your desire can lead you astray. If you ask too much you will not sell the property. If you ask too little you are being foolish. Buying and selling is not as cut and dried as this oversimplification may appear. Other factors may be involved.

Proper Timing Increases Profits

Another factor involved in the buying and selling of property is timing. Timing is the ability to buy or sell at the high or low of the market. Having the feel of timing is an ability that is achieved through long experience and keeping in constant touch with buyers, sellers and lending institutions. These qualifications are found in competent real estate investment brokers or real estate investment counselors.

An interesting case comes to mind that took place in a Long Island town. However, this particular situation also occurred all over America with similar results. For a great many years the main shopping area in this Long Island town was the traditional main street. Shoppers followed a prevalent pattern and fought to park in very limited parking spaces. The shoppers inconvenienced themselves because they had no other choice. After World War II there was a population explosion and the existing shopping, with dramatic suddenness, became obsolete.

My office had always had great success in leasing stores along this main street. We had a long list for any available stores. Property rarely changed hands along this street; it was generally closely held for generations.

Along about this time I had the feeling that something had to happen. I investigated with the local building department and discovered plans filed for four shopping centers within a radius of three miles. This in itself did not alarm me—except for one center, which was planned to be erected on 40 acres. A 40 acre center would contain an additional quantity of stores greater than the entire assemblage of main street stores. Plus, and a big plus, acres and acres of parking.

I was confident that the present was the time to sell. I approached a number of main street owners and recommended that they sell. All agreed that the time was ripe, except for one owner, the largest property holder in town. He absolutely refused to sell, stressing that what was good enough for his grandfather was good enough for him. I attempted to prove to him that he was in an exposed position, but that I could sell the property. I tried to make clear that there were still enough reactionaries about who vehemently believed that the future could be found in the past. These people were potential buyers; he still refused to sell.

The owners who agreed to sell were fortunate because despite being in potentially deep financial trouble they were able to sell their properties at inflated prices.

The big property owner still owns his property. As leases expired all of his individual chain tenants moved. In order to have some income he leased his stores for non-retail use—storage. As his gross rental dropped drastically, his real estate taxes rose dramatically. The profit margin slid downward, became a loss and continued to produce bigger and bigger losses.

Today, the property is for sale. At long last the big property owner has decided that he no longer wished to retain ownership of a property that appeared to have a dismal future. The property today can be purchased, just assume the present mortgage. The problem with this proposal is that the interest and amortization payments far exceed the income. This is a prime example of an owner who did not know when to sell.

Some years ago I met a young fellow whose father had died and left him a parking lot. This young fellow, Harry S. by name, had a burning desire to be a builder. To achieve this end he sold the parking lot for $30,000, purchased a piece of land, hired a contractor and built a taxpayer. With his $30,000 cash, a building loan and later a permanent mortgage he was able to complete the building. The stores were leased and Harry was delighted that he had built his own taxpayer and was earning a good living.

At this juncture I met Harry, who told me about his taxpayer. I looked at the property, analyzed it, and came to the conclusion that the stores were greatly over-rented; the tenants were paying too great a rental. It had been my experience that it was not difficult to lease at inflated rentals, but difficult to retain tenants if their business did not justify these rentals. Harry did not realize that he was actually in peril of being wiped out.

After considerable effort I managed to bring Harry to sell. I persuaded Harry that it was better to sell and be sorry than not to sell and be sorry. The taxpayer was sold and Harry doubled his money. He now had $60,000 in cash. With this money he continued building and today he is one of America's largest commercial builders.

About the first taxpayer that Harry built—it turned out to be a disaster. The tenants couldn't pay the rent and they all moved out. Finally, the bank foreclosed and rented at a considerably lower figure. The time to sell, in this situation, was of prime importance. If Harry had not sold when he did, one of the country's leading builders would have been bankrupt. A brilliant career would have been abruptly halted.

When to buy or when to sell is one of the most significant aspects of the investment business. Even if you are a professional, I still recommend an experienced investment counselor. I have the conviction that outside counsel is preferable because of the absence of personal involvement which can cloud even the best judgment.

The acquisition and sale of real estate is covered in many technical books, and is frequently explained with difficult economic theories. I do observe nevertheless that a prime cause for failure is on many occasions left out. Perhaps this "prime reason" is omitted because possibly, it doesn't fit into high sounding theories. I speak of greed. The little gremlin that quietly does its work—telling people that no matter how much an offer may be, they can do better.

Reasonable Sellers Make Good Profits

I once assembled a three acre parcel located in town. The property was to be used for a shopping center. The parking was to be in front, with the stores at the rear. I received options on all of the necessary properties except for a 25' x 100' piece.

The parcel I had not been able to acquire was located about ten feet below grade, improved with a 100 year old converted two family dwelling. Actually it was a shack. Two cousins, who had inherited the property, lived on the premises. The building had little worth—probably should have been condemned. The land was worth $3.00 a square foot, but being ten feet below grade substantially detracted from its value. Nevertheless, considering that this was the last parcel I offered the cousins $7,500. The offer was quickly rejected. I conferred with the purchasers and was told to offer a price that would entice the brothers into selling. My second offer was $25,000. The brothers told me that I wasn't even close; they wanted $100,000. I relayed the information to the buyers and they gave me a final offer of $75,000. Again I contacted the cousins who advised me that they had decided to ask $150,000. They were never contacted again. The shopping center was built around the cousins' property. The 2,500' lot was actually a depression in the shopping center parking lot. A cement block wall was built around three sides of the outer perimeter. The little old house still stands but it has practically no value whatsoever. The cousins through their greed lost all, instead of turning a handsome profit.

Inordinate and rapacious greed has been the downfall for many people. A typical story concerns a little old lady, whose husband, now dead, had been a real estate broker. The old lady owned a small, unimproved, one family site. The parcel was irregular and was worth perhaps $4,000. The parcel contained a total of 2,000 square feet. The old lady came to me, because I had been a friend of her husband. It seemed that a well known builder was erecting an apartment building adjacent to her property. In conjunction with the apartment building the builder was constructing a small children's playground. The old lady's parcel would round out the property. Actually, her parcel was not absolutely necessary, but would be helpful. I advised the old lady that the parcel would bring about $4,000 on the open market, but because of the builder's need I would try to get her the absolute top dollar. After a month of negotiation I finally convinced the builder to agree to a price of $25,000. Flushed with victory I called the little old lady and advised her that I had an offer of $25,000. The old lady told me that her attorney had advised her to not accept a penny less than $75,000. I told the little lady that if she or her attorney wished to negotiate with the builder they were at liberty to do so. The builder built his apartment building and also his playground. The playground was a little smaller than he would have liked, but perfectly adequate.

What happened to the little old lady? Nothing. She is still alive, still owns the property which is now worth perhaps $6,000. However, she has paid over $3,000 in taxes over the last 20 years.

Greed can affect both sellers and attorneys. You must rationalize and determine just how necessary your property is to the success of the complete project. You must also determine if the price you are asking is within limit. There always is a limit. Once you go beyond the limit you may endanger your transaction.

What To Look For

Real estate is a commodity that goes through cycles of change. These cycles historically occur over long periods of time, in many cases some twenty years apart. These periods of change are constantly occurring in different sectors. This restructuring can create wealth for you. The trick is in being able to recognize these changes.

How do we recognize the changes?

(A) Rent resistance. Tenants balking at increases.
(B) Old tenants failing to exercise options.
(C) Tenants' failure to refixture commercial units, redecorate apartments in residential units, and failure to renovate offices.

Items A, B and C are important because they are change trends. They warn you that the time to sell has arrived, if you own the property. Conversely, if you are an investor the change trend warns you not to buy.

When the same set of change trends are reversed—for example, tenants are paying rent increases, etc.—the opportunity for investment profit exists. The owner should hold his property for a good price and the prospective investor should try to purchase this type of investment.

There is still another trend to look for and this is a result trend. When there is no longer a change in progress, but rather a result, the following circumstances will be observed.

Vacancies
Numerous changes in tenancy
Evacuation of chain tenancy
Changes in character of neighborhood
Poor landlord maintenance
Functional obsolescence
Economical obsolescence

The result trend is best used to determine properties that are on a downward trend. Attention to this trend will be invaluable to both buyers and sellers.

7

Accumulating Wealth Through Net Leases

To start at the beginning, let us first define "net lease." A net lease is a lease containing the tenant's obligation to pay all expenses. Under today's generally accepted definition, "all expenses" does not include mortgage interest or amortization payments. However, "all expenses" does include the following:

Taxes   Water
Insurance   Sewer
Interior Repairs   Supplies, cleaning
Exterior Repairs   Utilities
  (to include structural)   All assessments

In effect, this leaves the landlord a carefree property with no expenses whatsoever. This type property is generally tenanted by a AAA-1 tenancy on a long term lease. In theory, this would be the safest and best type of property to own.

Good Tenancy Creates Safety

Now, let us carefully analyze a net lease offering. The property will usually be under a long term net lease to a well rated tenancy. Even with the long term lease we must pay much attention to the location. After all, 15-20 years is a long time and a location can, in this extended period, stand still, change for the better or change for the worse. It would seem that what we are really purchasing is possible future and safety. The safety should be guaranteed by the lease with the tenant. It must be because, in effect, you are buying a piece of paper.

We will cover those items contained in this piece of paper (lease) a little later. When you express an interest to brokers or owners by answering advertisements, you will receive listings of net leased property.

The illustration that follows is a typical net lease listing.

Illustration #3-1

(1)	Net Lease for Sale
(2)	Shows 10% free and clear
(3) LOCATION:	127 Main St., New York, N.Y.
(4) DESCRIPTION:	One story brick building of 3,000 sq. ft.
(5) PLOT:	6,000 sq. ft.
(6) FINANCING:	Free and Clear
(7) LEASE:	20 years (originally)
(8) RENT:	(Net) $5000
(9) EXPENSES:	Paid by tenant none
(10) CASH FLOW:	$5000
(11) PRICE:	$50,000 to show 10% net.
(12) REMARKS:	Property is two years old. 10 car on-premises parking.
(13) ABOUT TENANT:	Tenant is rated AAA-1 ($80,000,000 net worth). Tenant has been established 20 years.

Subject to error, omission, prior sale or withdrawal. All without notice.

Some net lease listings contain a little more or less information, but this information is about what you would find in an average listing.

Dissecting A Listing

The first two lines are lead lines that have a main function of attracting your attention. Line #3 is self explanatory in that it tells where the property is located.

Well Located—A Must

The location of a net leased property is very important, even more so than with other types of property. The reason for this is that net leased property has a smaller return and we strive to make this up by eventually having valuable land—that is, land that has accrued in value during the term of the lease. If the building also helps to increase the value, so much the better, but this usually does not happen. After 15 years the building will probably be outmoded. Most net leased properties contain specialty type buildings which become outmoded within 15-20 years or less.

Try to purchase a property that is not in the heart of town. Do not buy the so called 100% location, the one surrounded by all the big chain stores. Within one economic cycle (15-20 years), the 100% area will move. It is important that you purchase your property within the path of this progress. Consequently, you will have purchased property at a reduced price (as compared to properties in the 100% area) and have an opportunity to achieve an increase in the value of your property of 3-500%. Remember to place yourself in the path of future commercial progress.

Improvement Of Little Importance

Line 4, description, is a description of the improvement upon the property. As I have previously stated, the building is of little importance when planning future growth of your property. The building, will, in most cases, be a specialty type property and probably completely outmoded by the end of the lease.

100' x 200' Minimum Plot

Item #5 is the plot. With on-premises parking continually gaining in importance, it is imperative that your plot be at least 200' in depth. A 200' depth permits front parking, with the building set back. The width of a property will vary, depending upon its particular use. However, regardless of use, 100' should be your minimum width. Do not purchase a property with a 100' x 100' plot. This is an outmoded size and it will not accrue in value as greatly as a parcel with 200' in depth and a frontage with a minimum of 100'.

Item #6 is financing. In this case, the property is free and clear. If you are planning to carry the property free and clear then you have no problem. However, if you plan to finance the property and thus cut down on your invested cash then this may be done. Financing will be discussed in greater detail in another chapter.

Fifteen Years Or Better—A Must

Item #7 is the length of the lease. Fifteen years should be the minimum accepted term. If within a few years you should decide that you want to finance the property, you would have problems with a shorter lease. The ideal lease is for 25 years. This term lends itself to choice financing. Also, less than 15 years may not be enough time for changes that may take place to enhance your property's value.

Is The Property Over-Rented?

Item #8 is the rent, which is not too important. After all, you are getting a return on invested cash. If the rent is greater, your investment is greater. If the rent is lower, then conversely, your investment is lower. The only real pitfall to avoid is a property that is grossly over-rented. If a property rental is worth $5,000 per annum, then we do not want to purchase this type property with a rental of $10,000. You will not only be paying double its value, but will be destroying part of its future.

The problem then comes up, how do you determine proper rental? Speak with local brokers who are familiar with rental values. Remember, I said brokers, not lawyers. Commercial brokers are experts in this field and can show you comparable properties and thereby give you proper advice. There may be some lawyers who can advise a client regarding these rentals, but they would be few and far between. See local real estate brokers for the proper information.

Tenant Pays All

Item #9, expenses, may be a little tricky. Many properties are offered for sale as net properties. Make sure that all, and I do mean *all,* expenses are the responsibility of the tenant, (referred to in leases as the lessee). The tenant, or lessee, should be responsible for:

(A) All taxes	(E) Insurance, including
(B) All assessments	rent, fire and liability
(C) Interior repairs	(F) Maintenance
(D) Exterior repairs,	(G) Water/Sewer
including structural	(H) Supplies, cleaning
	(I) Utilities

Item #10, cash flow, speaks for itself. If the net lease is a pure net lease, free and clear of financing, then the rental paid by the tenant is in effect also the cash flow.

Item #11, the price, is that price agreed upon between buyer and seller. The price when used as a ratio with the cash flow will create your percentage of yield.

Item #12, remarks, serves as a catchall section within which all miscellaneous information has been listed. Any details that do not quite fit under the other headings will find themselves listed under this heading.

Item #13, about the tenant, should merely serve to introduce you to the tenant. I suggest that you call the offices of the tenant and request a copy of their latest statement. If your tenant is a public company (one that sells its stock to the public, and is listed over-the-counter, New York Stock Exchange or American Stock Exchange), they will promptly comply with your request. If the company is not a public company and will not issue a proper statement, then you should not buy the deal.

Who Signed The Lease

After you receive the tenant's statement, you should have your accountant advise you regarding the stability of the company. And now for a very important item. Who actually signed the lease? Make sure that the name on the lease is the tenant's parent company. Many of the larger firms have subsidiary firms with quite modest net worths. These companies do not always bind the parent to the lease obligation, the exception being where the parent will agree to guarantee performance of a lease signed by a subsidiary company.

Now that the listing has been carefully gone over, if you are satisfied, then engage an attorney to go over the lease and the attending contract of sale.

Additional Points

In a previous chapter, I outlined "Typical Investment Yields," and categorized net leases as governed by the prime rate. This is true as far as it goes. However, net leases are different from other types of investment properties. Net leases are, for practical purposes, real estate guaranteed by a piece of paper (the lease). The strength of the company signing the lease governs the yield—starting with a minimum yield of ½% below the prime rate. The schedule of returns on equity (on a free & clear basis) is as follows:

YIELD*	COMPANIES RATING, NET WORTH
9½%	100 Million and greater
10%	80 Million
10¼%	60 Million
10½%	40 Million
11%	20 Million
11¼%	10 Million
11%—13½%	5 Million and less

*Based on prime rate of 10%

We frequently hear the cliche, "There is nothing new in real estate." Not true. In 1964 mini-warehouses came into being. Within the next few years the conception caught hold and now there are mini-warehouses all the way to California.

With numerous homes being erected with partial or no basements, storage has become a problem. Also, with our country growing in affluence personal items grow and families add boats, trailers, campers, etc. These items must be stored someplace and mini-warehouses fill the bill.

The mini-warehouse is constructed of both wood and metal. The trend today is heavily in favor of metal, with the exterior covered with preservatives that give the look of masonry. The building is divided into rental spaces running from 50 square feet to 600 square feet. All units have outside, individual doors; each lessee has his own key to his space. Warehouse firms, experienced in the field, manage and operate the mini-warehouses. Tenants may come and go during the daylight hours. The exterior perimeter is surrounded by chain link fences and the entire area is patrolled with adequate security.

The warehouses are built and leased to operating firms on a long term net basis. Then the property is sold on a net lease basis. The yields for the mini-warehouses are quite good. Twenty five percent cash is required with the balance being financed. The usual yield on equity is 11% plus amortization. For investors interested in new ideas in net leases the mini-warehouse complexes are good alternatives.

One of the more interesting aspects of the net lease is the sale-leaseback. The sale-leaseback, for certain people, has a clear edge over the net lease. The net lease, for practical purposes, is a locked-in situation. The net lease yield is historically minimal. However, with the sale-leaseback there is an opportunity to achieve an unusually large yield with an excellent limit of safety. The sale-leaseback may be made with an improved property, with the land beneath the property, or both land and building may be net leased together, or the building alone may be net-leased.

The land sale-leaseback is a substantially simple operation in that the owner of the fee retains the ownership of the improvement, but no longer owns the land. The original owner sells the land to a purchaser then net leases the property on a long term basis. The lessee pays all expenses. Almost any type of investment property is well suited to a sale-leaseback situation. The safety hedge in the land lease is for the improvement to generate enough income to be able to pay two times the ground rental. It should be noted that while ordinary net leases generally run for a period of fifteen to twenty years, the land lease will run for some forty to ninety-nine years. The land leases will, in a great many cases, contain options with cost of living increases built in.

Up to this point I have covered everything except the risk factor. Suppose the tenant goes bad—what happens? From a practical standpoint, not very much. The land is generally subordinated to a mortgage. The financing is subject to the land lease and this factor invariably produces minimum financing. This is done in order to create a good take-over situation. If the land owner has to take over in the event of a lease default his expenses will be less than that of the previous tenant. The land owner saves the price of the land rental. Also, the building now becomes the property of the land owner who now owns both land and building. The acquisition of the building is quite a coup, because the land owner usually pays about 50% of the property's value when purchasing the land. The yield on equity is generally between 9% and 11%. Now to reconstruct—if the property is acquired for 50% of its value, subject to financing, and if the land rent is eliminated then the property has less expense and the new owner is in a position to accept less rent. The margin of safety is very good.

The more popular net type of sale is the sale-leaseback. The entire property is purchased and then leased back to the seller. Great fortunes have been made in this type operation. Almost all of the transactions are large deals. However, I know a chap, Bob E., who has done exceptionally well handling small deals only. One particular deal that comes to mind was a small neighborhood taxpayer with a cash flow of $4,500. Bob offered 10% to investors (actually, the property threw off 12%). Ten investors purchased at the $30,000 offered. Bob had paid $37,000 for the property. With only $7,000 left in the job he was making $1,500 per annum, which gave Bob 21% on his investment. In addition Bob received 50% of any amortization profits. Last I heard, Bob had over twenty of these small leasebacks in operation. The sale-leaseback lends itself to both large and small operations.

What To Look For

1. A true net lease makes all expenses the obligation of the tenant.
2. Your location must be within the path of future expansion.
3. Good tenancy creates safety.
4. Don't overemphasize the importance of the property improvement.
5. 100′ depth properties are outmoded. 200′ depth should be a minimum.
6. Leases must be for a minimum of 15 years.
7. Be careful of over-rented properties.
8. Check the company on the lease.

8

Avoiding Tax Pitfalls

Basically the investor of today is sophisticated enough to understand that mere return, or cash flow, does not tell the whole story. Within the laws that govern the taxation of real estate income there are a number of avenues that, in varying degrees, shelter taxable income and aid in avoiding tax pitfalls that could prove expensive.

One of the methods is the division of income. With a permanent asset such as real estate, the taxable income may be divided among members of the immediate family including children, grandchildren, etc. The income may also be divided by giving gifts. The giving of a gift, say to a minor child who has no other income, may greatly reduce a father's tax liability.

Achieving tax advantages is not a one way street, but rather one with relatively numerous and unlikely avenues. Investors seek different types of favorable advantages in order to aid individual tax liability problems.

Keogh Act Benefits

A prevalent tax shelter scheme is called the Keogh Act, so named after Congressman Keogh who initiated the bill. Fundamentally the law was enacted to aid individuals who operate unincorporated businesses of their own. Those covered would include doctors, lawyers, trades people, professional people, etc.

The working of the Keogh Act is moderately unmixed. To be more explicit, not only the self-employed boss, but also the employees may be covered by the Keogh Act. The employer may contribute 10% of his income or $2,500 per annum, whichever is less. The monies are used toward the funding of a retirement trust. Employees included in the plan must work over twenty-hours per week and have been employed at least three years.

The investment of funds may be in real estate. With a maximum of $2,500 per annum it will not be possible to purchase large properties, but there are any number of syndication shares that may be purchased. The funds may be withdrawn in either of two ways—either in a lump sum or in installments. Both procedures have good tax shelter. If withdrawn in a lump sum the monies may be averaged over five years. If the alternate method, installments, is elected it is assumed that at that time the recipient will be in a lower tax bracket and the income is taxed as regular income. The monies may not be withdrawn until age 59½ and must be withdrawn at age 70½.

An often-used tax deduction is the installment sale. Here the seller usually takes 29% cash and the balance in the form of a mortgage. In this way the taxable income is spread out over a period of years, thereby reducing the tax liability.

Trades Create Important Shelters

One of the most complicated, and much-used tax shelters, is the trade or exchange. The foundation for this entire system is dependent upon the I.R.S. definition of "like kind." Like kind, in an oversimplification, applies to real estate being exchanged for real estate. This distinctive type of trade is indispensable in order to effect a tax free exchange.

When I refer to trading real estate I am including all types. For example, vacant land for improved property. This is considered a trade of like properties. An exchange of real estate for personal property is not covered under the like kind definition. To carry the definition even further, the exchange fundamentally eliminates receiving cash from a sale, the money being immediately subject to a tax. In the trade mode there is created a postponement of capital gains and a continuity of cash flow.

A tax free interchange must have the imperative requirement of an exchange and not a sale in order to sustain the benefit from a tax free reciprocal transference position. At any time, if a property is sold and then there is effected a third party substitution there has not been a legitimate trade. This has been a sale and subsequently it will be taxable. When an exchange actually does take place it is not always nontaxable; it may be partially taxable. I must explain that when I use the term nontaxable, it may be nontaxable at present—a deferred tax.

An additional factor to be taken into consideration is who is involved in the transaction. A dealer cannot be involved in a tax free exchange. The I.R.S. definition of a dealer is one who inventories properties for resale to clients.

An interesting exchange is one that occurred on the following basis. John B. owned a thirty-two family apartment building for some ten years. John B. wanted to sell his building and purchase a larger building. I showed him a forty-family building that he liked—and eventually he decided that he wanted to buy it. There was a problem. While John B. desired to trade up, he did not have the cash to cover the additional equity. The two buildings, using an oversimplified listing, shaped up as follows:

	John B.'s Building	Other Property
Fair market value	$72,000	$135,000
Financing	$12,500	$ 50,000
Cash Equity	$59,500	$ 85,000
Cash to Seller		$ 25,500

Based upon the listing, John B. would require the difference in cash equities, $25,500, in order to be able to acquire the property he desired. The disposition of things allowed that in order to make the deal the mortgage on the "other" property be refinanced in the amount of $75,500. The new mortgage created a cash equity of $59,500 for each property. Both parties agreed and a tax free exchange was made. The aim of a great many traders is to trade up without the expenditure of cash to cover the seller's equity. In many situations this can be accomplished.

The ways and means used to achieve trades are endless. A builder I knew came to me and asked me to inquire if a certain vacant business lot was for sale. The lot was situated in Tucson, Arizona, and well-located. I searched the records and found that the lot had been purchased some 20 years previous for $2,500. The original purchaser had died and his son now owned the property. It was now worth $30,000. I approached the owner and was informed that the builder had previously contacted the son and had been told that the property was not available. The son was greatly concerned about a capital gains tax, which would have been substantial. Furthermore he felt that his property had a great future and would continue to enhance in value. After a number of conversations I convinced him that as vacant land this property was peaking out. I then spoke "trade" to him and he appeared to have interest since he did not have to put in any additional cash.

I located a drive-in restaurant, on a large plot, that was for sale. The property was out of the action, but in the growth path. This was a property that had a remarkable opportunity to enhance in value over the next few years. The tenant's rental was low and consequently the sales price was a reasonable $30,000. The builder purchased the drive-in property and in turn traded with the son who owned the original vacant parcel. The reason that the builder had to make a purchase and trade was because the owner of the drive-in did not want to trade. He wanted cash. The way the deal worked out is as follows:

(A) Drive-in owner—wanted cash and received same.
(B) Builder—wanted vacant lot and traded for same.
(C) "Son"—wanted to trade for a parcel with a future with no cash outlay—he traded for what he wanted.
(D) Broker—delighted to have made three commissions.

Real estate traditionally has always been the recipient of preferred tax shelter. The revised 1969 tax act reduced the tax shelter somewhat, but it still did not remove real estate from its status as one of the superior tax shelter investments.

Taking proper advantage of legitimate tax shelters is of vast importance. The use of an improper method in buying or selling may be a dangerous tax pitfall.

What To Look For

Owning a profitable parcel of real estate is nice. It is even nicer when the cash flow is partially or completely tax free. It is important to determine, when purchasing, if a property offered with alleged tax advantages actually possesses these advantages.

There are a number of "no" situations that are tax pitfalls and must be avoided. Some that occur most frequently are the following:

(A) If an installment sale is made with 29% cash it must be remembered that the interest charges on the remaining balance will, during the first year, possibly increase the cash to over 29%. This will destroy a tax advantage.

(B) In a trade situation, where cash is involved, that portion is not tax sheltered.

(C) If a trade is made by a dealer it will be disallowed. Dealers may not be involved in tax sheltered exchanges.

(D) Avoid third party substitutions, as these are considered sales, not trades.

(E) Keep in mind that many so-called tax free shelters are not tax free, but rather tax deferred.

9

Creating Wealth Through Office Buildings

Office buildings fall into a number of categories. However, the basics always remain the same. The return (cash flow) is generally a higher yield than for many other types of property, the reason being that office buildings contain a large risk factor.

Within the past several years I have seen a fair amount of small office buildings erected. These buildings are usually specialty types. I refer to medical and professional buildings. These buildings represent only a small segment of the office building market—a market, that because of its high risk factor, is to a large degree built, maintained, managed and leased by sophisticated professionals. The large office building still controls over 90% of the market and shows no signs of slipping.

Following you will note an office building listing, Illustration 10-1. Refer to this listing as I carefully go through it.

Location, The Investment Foundation

Location is important because to a large degree it controls the rental market. With any office location there are only three choices and a number of intermediate degrees. The options are:

Choice location	90% to 100%
Medium location	60% to 89%
Poor location	59% or less

The reason for rating locations by degrees, as 90%, 80%, etc., is because a choice location, for example, may be fantastic or it may be on the fringe and almost ready to fall into the medium location group. On the other hand, a changing neighborhood may increase a poor location of say 60% to perhaps 80%. We must have a degree method for determining choice, medium and poor locations. This is a relatively simple matter of inquiring as to the present rentals within a reasonable area (5-6 miles radius*). The rental values are then placed into the three categories with the highest 10% being choice, the next 29% being medium and the balance being rated as poor.

Securing the degree of each classification is a little more difficult. Your best source is a real estate broker—not just any realty broker, but one who is a specialist in the management of office buildings. Have the broker prepare a rental survey of similar office buildings in this city over a period of five years. An analysis of the rentals will easily create a pattern of increases, decreases, or static rentals. The speed with which the rentals change is also the speed with which the rental value in the area is changing. If you do not wish to consult a realty broker, you may consult the local registrar's office where many leases are recorded, and you should be able to create a rental pattern. The purchase money mortgage referred to will be explained fully later in this chapter.

Be Aware Of Rental Patterns

The rental pattern is most important in that it can give a prospective purchaser a glimpse into the future. A rental pattern will

---

*Refers to urban locations. Suburban locations would be greater.

Illustration 10-1

Grant Building
Omaha, Nebraska

LOCATION: S/W corner Main St. and 10th Ave.

PLOT SIZE: 125' x 125': Built—125' x 115'.

DESCRIPTION: 11 story fireproof office building in the heart of the downtown business district. Three high speed manual elevators. Approximately 100% of the building has been air-conditioned. Tenancies include The Federal Land Bank (8 floors), N.Y. Life Assurance Society and California Mutual Life Insurance Co.

RENTABLE
AREA: 11 floors of offices. 90,000 sq. ft.

1st MORTGAGE: $764,000 (originally $800,000) payable $72,000 per annum, including 7% interest. Due 10 years. Institutional.

ESTIMATED INCOME:	Offices	$360,000	
	Electricity & Misc'l.	6,000	$366,000

ESTIMATED EXPENSES:	Interest & amortization,		
	1st Mtge.	$ 72,000	
	Real Estate Taxes	46,200	
	Water & sewer	2,200	
	Insurance	3,010	
	Oil	11,000	
	Payroll & payroll taxes	27,500	
	Electricity	20,000	
	Maintenance	18,000	
	Cleaning	25,000	
	Management	10,000	$234,910

ESTIMATED CASH FLOW: $131,090

PRICE: $950,000 over financing, terms.

Illustration 10-1 (continued)

Rent Roll
Grant Building—Omaha, Nebraska

Tenant	Lease Exp. Date	Size	Rental
*Federal Land Bank	11 years	72,000'	$287,000
*N.Y. Life Assurance Society	10 years	4,000'	16,000
*California Mutual Life Ins. Co.	9 years	3,000'	12,000
Paris Exporters	4 years	500'	2,700
Kansas Finance Co.	6 years	500'	2,700
*British Insurance Co.	9 years	2,000'	8,000
Equitable Insurance Co.	7 years	500'	2,700
Jon Jacque	7 years	200'	1,200
John Doe	8 years	200'	1,200
Harry Smith	5 years	100'	500
Nebraska Architectural Co.	9 years	1,500'	7,500
Dr. A.B. Gilbert	6 years	1,500'	7,500
Dr. H.M. Greene	8 years	2,000'	8,500
*AAA Oil Co.	11 years	2,000'	8,500
		90,000'	$366,000

*AAA-1 Companies.

<u>Author's note:</u> While the per square foot average is slightly over $4.00, some of the smaller tenants are paying up to $6.00 per sq. ft. This is usual for smaller spaces.

Those companies designated with an asterisk are rated AAA-1 firms with the parent companies guaranteeing the leases. AAA-1 income totals $331,500. Your total expense including a P.M. 2nd mortgage is $266,410. The AAA-1 tenancy are all on leases running between 9-11 years. From a safety standard, the building is a good investment. However, other factors must still be considered.

Subject to errors, omission, prior sale or withdrawal. All without notice.

follow a true economic cycle. The cycle ordinarily will run for approximately twenty years. This cycle can be broken by unusual happenings. Some of these unusual happenings are:

1. Re-routing of major streets.
2. Changes in building style.
3. Offstreet parking created elsewhere.
4. Major companies vacating the area.
5. Merchandising changes which may shift business districts.
6. Overproduction.
7. Neighborhood downgrading.

The re-routing of streets can occur in major cities and also in small towns. A small town may, in some instances, be badly hurt economically when a thruway is built by-passing the town. The erection of a thruway may change the thinking of major companies. Large cities have much the same problems, but to a lesser degree. Crosstown expressways built to meet at other forms of transportation such as bridges, subways, etc., may cause a major change. Municipal changes do not occur with any great speed, often taking many years to occur. A visit to the planning department of any city will provide you with all the information you require relative to proposed changes.

The Building May Be Outmoded

Changes in building styles do not occur very often, but when they do, they may be major. Examples of major changes would be central air-conditioning, high speed elevators, garages in buildings, etc. Changes of this type can occur with suddenness. One builder may place a new innovation into his structure and create an immediate tenant demand in the entire industry for this item. The best method of meeting sudden change is to prepare for this change in advance. As one of your expense items, you must create a sinking fund of 10% of your cash flow as an anticipation item, which will offset possible major changes.

Off street parking is a prime asset to any office building. If a hypothetical building is located in an older town, where because of improper planning years ago, there is no parking, it would be equal to all the other buildings in town. However, if the municipality decided to upgrade its town by the establishment of off street parking in a distant area, it could economically damage the other areas. Establishment of off street parking in commercial areas takes years to happen. The procedure involves negotiation, condemnation, court fights, and demolition. A visit to the city planning commission will alert you to municipality future plans. The information is public and will be dispensed at your request.

Major companies have a habit of being clannish, in that they attempt to locate space in buildings containing other major firms in the same line of business. Airlines, buying offices, and insurance companies are the leaders. This habit of following one another can cause major vacancies and consequently loss of revenue. The trend has always been to move to new, more modern buildings and a willingness to pay greater rentals for these facilities. When contemplating a purchase, it is important to carefully inspect the rental tenancy list in order to check lease expiration dates. Your major tenancy must be on long term leases. If not, you must prepare, to be safe, for possible vacancy prospects. Calculate what the space will rerent for. This can be done by comparison with similar buildings. Have a contractor advise what modernization of the vacated space will cost. Calculate brokerage fee for rerental. I attach great importance to this, because the cost may be considerable. Let me show you an example:

Old Rental	$10,000
New Rental	8,000
Yearly loss	$ 2,000

Net loss @ 10 years	$20,000	
Contractors estimate*	8,000	
Brokerage, 10 yr. lease	2,600	
Total Loss		$30,600.

*Note: One year's rent for remodeling is average.

A 20% dip in rental can be very costly. There is also the possibility, which I have not calculated, of the space being vacant for an extended period. This of course would increase the total loss figure. We provide for this contingency by either not buying the building or making a proper allowance in price.

Merchandise Changes Cause Vacancies

Merchandise changes do not occur often, and when they do, many signs point to a forthcoming change. The only true major merchandising change to affect office building in many years has been the tendency to erect free standing drive-in type buildings. The free standing buildings are erected on the outside fringes of a town. Transportation facilities are completely ignored, except for the automobile. The shift begins with the erection of small buildings and is followed by large office buildings and lastly by free standing retail shops. Drive about the fringes of the town and look for small office buildings. From the first building of small office buildings to the shift to retail stores, you have a period of perhaps 20 years. Using 20 years as your time guide and observing the amount of suburban building, you can easily gauge how many years remain before the old office building sector suffers from obsolescence.

Overproduction is self-explanatory. If you see many vacancies in new buildings then the production of buildings has outpaced the demand and created a saturated market. This situation may eventually adjust itself, but your waiting for this event may be expensive. I recommend that you avoid this type of situation.

Neighborhood downgrading is a sort of slow death. It occurs over a period of years. The classic symptoms are physical deterioration of buildings, obsolescence, successive degeneration, and the invasion of low end commercial enterprises.

In discussing the "unusual happenings" that can break an economic cycle, I have stated that any of these happenings occur over an extended period of time. This should not lull you into a false sense of security. The building you are contemplating purchasing may be in the 4th, 8th or even 18th year of a happening. Careful study is indicated.

Plot Size—Shape Means Dollars

The plot size of an office building, to my mind presents only two problems: Its shape and easements. If a plot is either square or rectangular it is, when remodeling, more economical than an irregular plot. It is possible by intricate appraisal methods to prove different plots more valuable than others. However, for the man purchasing an office building his only concern is the buildings present and the future ability to produce adequate income. Inquire from the seller, or his broker, if there are any easement restrictions. Determine if the easements, if any, are detrimental to future leasing, financing or selling.

Description, a Major Category

The description in the average listing may cover four or five lines. In effect it tells little or nothing. However, it is of major importance. A description actually should, but rarely does, contain the following:

1. Floor plan of each floor containing arrangement of halls, lavatories and hallways.
2. Adequate description and condition of air-conditioning, heating system and plumbing.
3. Adequate lighting survey.
4. Are hung ceilings required?
5. Condition and age of elevators.
6. Condition of incinerators, motors, pumps, dynamos, transformers, sprinkler system.
7. Is lobby modern or does it require renovation?

I don't say that you should immediately hire people to check out the mechanical parts of the building. First, make sure of everything else. If you are ready to purchase a property, subject to the mechanical equipment being in good working order, then you should hire experts to survey that equipment.

The balance of the items covering layout, lighting, ceilings, etc. may be checked by yourself, with a physical inspection or if you wish expert opinion, bring along a realty management expert. Generally there will be no charge for his services.

Rentable Area—Must Be Adequate

The rentable area is, of course, the net area left after taking out hallways, stairwells, lavatories, lobbies, etc. Check to make sure that you will not have to widen halls or enlarge lavatories in order to maintain a modern building. If this area is not adequate, you will have to reduce the rentable area and thereby reduce your projected gross rental.

First Mortgage—Can It Be Refinanced?

The first mortgage was originally $800,000. The mortgage has been reduced to $704,000 or approximately 12%. Checking a mortgage table, "constant annual percent," we note that the mortgage was written for a 15 year period and 5 years have already expired. When the mortgage reaches maturity in 10 years, or 15 years from its inception, approximately 53% of the principal will have been amortized. Therefore the balance will be $376,000.

At this point I feel it necessary to get ahead of myself. Later in this chapter I explain a purchase money mortgage taken back by the owner. The P.M. mortgage is in the amount of $350,000 at 6% interest and 3% amortization. The P.M. mortgage will be due at the same time as the first mortgage. Referring to my "constant annual percent" mortgage chart, it is found that at the end of ten years, 41% of the mortgage will be paid off. This would make the P.M. mortgage balance $206,500.

Our total mortgage balance now is:

1st mortgage balance	$376,000
P.M. 2nd mortgage balance	206,500
Total mortgages	$582,500

The property requires refinancing at this point. Assuming that all things have remained static—rentals, mortgage terms, neighborhood, etc.—there will be no problem securing a new first mortgage in the original amount of $800,000.

Proposed new 1st mortgage		$800,000
Balance due old 1st Mtge.	$376,000	
Balance due old 2nd Mtge.	206,500	$582,500
Overage		$217,500

The mortgage overage is pocketed by the owner. Refinancing is one of the great benefits of investing. Consequently, it is of vital importance that when purchasing a property, we must try to get into an area that will improve, or at least remain static for 10-15 years. In a downgraded area the refinancing benefits would be on a sliding scale from less all the way down to nothing.

Estimated Income Must Be Verified

The estimated income is derived from office rentals (store space when present), sale of electricity and miscellaneous items such as income from telephones. The income must be checked against existing leases. If there are any new leases, check to see that they are in line with other leases. If the new leases show very substantial increases, then there are two possibilities to investigate.

First, the area may be increasing in value and the increases are warranted. This is easily checked by inquiring in competitive buildings as to their rentals. If the competition is asking rentals far below your new leases then beware.

The second possibility becomes a reality. The building has been "salted." A "salted" building is one that has re-rented its vacancies at a rental lower than the previous rental, but appears to have a greater rental. Let me illustrate.

Old rental	$8,000 per annum
New rental	6,000 per annum
Actual cash loss	$2,000 per annum

A lease may be signed with a new tenant showing a rental of $9,000 per annum for say 3 years. Actually the tenant has been given twelve months' concession. The breakdown is as follows:

Face of lease	$27,000	(3 years)
12 months concession	9,000	
Actual net rental	$18,000	(3 years)
	or $ 6,000 per annum	

The logical question is what's in it for the tenant and why is the tenant so cooperative? To begin with, the tenant has leased space at what would be fair market price. The inducement is the landlord's paying for office renovations or office fixtures. The net result of the "salting" has been to increase the rent roll by approximately 12% when actually the rent roll decreased by 25%. The landlord has actually bridged a gap of 35%.

Estimated Expenses—Fatten Them Up

Estimated expenses are, for the most part, calculated on the lean side. Every seller wants to make his building appear attractive and "estimated expenses" is the best place to achieve this goal.

Ordinarily we have approximately 10 or 11 items listed under expenses. In this case we have no second or purchase money mortgage. As we get further along we will create secondary financing, but for the present we will omit this expense.

Interest and amortization on the first mortgage is a cut and dried situation and may be taken on faith. The mortgage agreement will be exhibited at contract and so this item cannot be changed in any manner.

Real estate taxes are somewhat in the same category as mortgage payments. Ask for the latest tax bill and you have the correct figure. Some sellers attempt to present old tax figures, but this is a futile exercise as a new tax bill exposes the ploy.

Water and sewer is again a cut and dried item in that the latest bill tells the whole story.

Insurance is an important matter. Sometimes policies are deliberately omitted in order to reduce the expense figure. However, this is not always the case, as some owners, without realizing it, are underinsured. Being underinsured makes the owner, in the event of a loss, a co-insurer, thus reducing his interest in the loss. Ask for the seller's schedule of insurance. Present these figures to your own insurance broker and he will advise you relative to the coverage. There is generally no charge for this service.

Oil is a tricky item. The oil bill can vary depending upon the type of weather that existed during the past year. An owner may present you with bonafide bills and yet next year the heating bill could be greater or lesser. However, with legitimate fuel bills, it will average out to a true figure. To be doubly sure, you may call a fuel company and request an estimate of a year's requirements for this building. There is generally no charge for this service, and it will serve to confirm the original amount designated.

Payroll is generally correct. The seller will show you his operating statement submitted with his income tax return and you have the correct figure. If the building contains union help, speak with the union who will then advise you relative to the number of employees needed, the wage scale and the contract benefits.

Electricity, like a few of the other items, is easily determined. Bills for the prior twelve months will present you with the true expense.

Maintenance is a substantial figure and the one generally reduced significantly. Maintenance involves many items, each differing from year to year. Consequently, we cannot request a paid "bill" for maintenance from the landlord for the previous year. There are some methods used to arrive at reasonable results. When looking for property to purchase, you will undoubtedly have received listings of a number of properties. Compare the maintenance figures of similar buildings and arrive at a reasonably high figure. Another way to check is by the formula method. For large office buildings, we take 5% of the gross income and attribute that to maintenance. This formula used with comparable listings will give you a reasonably accurate accounting. There are other formulas sometimes used to determine expenses, but as you will note, I have avoided them completely. The formulas have not been given because they vary so widely in different geographic sectors. Only a very few formulas are able to survive the weight of geography.

Cleaning—A Major Expense

Cleaning, again, is a weighty expense and all possible care should be exercised to determine the correct figure. We must establish exactly how much cleaning you as the landlord may be responsible for. There is no question about the halls, lavatories, and lobby. These items are always the landlord's responsibility. Cleaning is generally supplied to all tenants in any substantial buildings (over 10,000'). Cleaning also includes floor waxing. Some tenants may receive this service while other tenants will not. The service or lack of service is reflected in their rental. After you have determined from consultation with the owner and inspection of leases the amount of service, you will be apprised of the number of square feet that will require waxing and polishing and the area that must be cleaned and dusted. Any local maintenance company will be happy to give you a free estimate. Of course if the building is already under a maintenance contract you need only inspect the contract to determine the maintenance cost. Do be careful about old contracts about to expire. We live in a world of increases and building maintenance is not exempt. If the contract has, or is about to expire, you will then require an estimate from a maintenance firm.

Management may be defined as the operation of a building to include a good leasing record, and a building that is both in good repair and clean. A well-managed building is an asset for any owner. The well-managed property has great intrinsic value in that its "eye appeal" will help to sell the building, or if not for sale, will provide pride of ownership. The cost of management varies from 2% to 5% depending upon geography and the size of the building. Those properties under 10,000 square feet will cost a 5% management fee. The larger properties command a 4% fee. Again, there will be some variances depending upon the individual locality.

"Estimated" cash flow is used instead of cash flow because for the prospective purchaser, the expense figures presented are true estimates. The year to year running costs of a building will vary. Sometimes the variance will be slight and at other times great. However, the expenses will generally average out, over a period of time, to correct estimates. The word estimate is also used to prevent a lawsuit. A purchaser may sue, claiming that his cash flow is less than he was led to believe. The word estimated tends to eliminate any future legal gymnastics.

Price is, of course, the name of the game. Price can make almost all buildings good. There are almost no bad buildings at the right price. Assuming that the subject listed building (Illustration 10-1) is entirely correct, we then have a cash flow of $131,000 (rounded). The price is $950,000 cash over the first mortgage financing with terms. The amount of cash that an investor should put into a building is as little as possible. Over the years both buyers and sellers have agreed on certain elastic formulas that apply equally as well in all parts of the country. Cash equity should be between one and two times the gross rental. Taking a figure within this range (1.6 x gross rental) we can reasonably assume that $600,000 cash will be acceptable to the seller and create a fair equity for the purchaser. The listing stipulates "terms," and so we can offer a purchase money mortgage for the balance. Every purchaser must realize that a P.M. mortgage is a mortgage of convenience created to reduce cash equity and also to create a greater net profit. A seller can, without dropping his price, create a favorable deal through the use of advantageous P.M. mortgage terms. The interest rate will often be below the then existing rate in order to increase the net yield. The P.M. 2nd mortgage will run between 10-15 years. I have seen some stubborn sellers insist on P.M. 2nd mortgages of from 1 to 5 years. Only an unsophisticated investor will buy a building with this type of mortgage. In five years or less the amortization on this mortgage will be almost nothing. When the mortgage is due the purchaser will have to pay off the mortgage, which in effect means buying the building all over again. Many sellers need cash and have in mind to sell the P.M. second mortgage. They, of course, will fight rather vigorously for a ten rather than a fifteen year mortgage—the difference in value being approximately 15%. In this case, a mortgage of $350,000 would represent, if sold as a ten year mortgage instead of a 15 year mortgage, a loss of $42,500 in additional mortgage discount. With this in mind a reasonable offer would be $350,000

P.M. second mortgage at 6% interest and 3% amortization, due in 10 years. Our offer analyzed will be as follows:

1. Cash flow (presently)		$131,000
2. Proposed P.M. 2nd mortgage. $350,000 at 6% interest and 3% amortization. Due in 10 years.		31,500
3. Net profit after paying interest and amortization on 1st mortgage and P.M. 2nd mortgage.		99,500
4. 10% cash flow sinking fund		9,950
		$ 89,550

5. Cash invested over both mortgages
   $600,000 = 15% yield on equity.

This transaction has been based upon an ordinary seller's P.M. second mortgage. There is, however, another type of P.M. second mortgage known as the operator's mortgage. In order to best illustrate a hypothetical situation, I will ask you to accept certain assumptions—assumptions that will appear often in everyday transactions.

Assume: (Principal)

   P.M. Mortgage of $100,000.

Proposal: (terms)

   6% interest and "O" amortization for 4 years.
   6% interest and 3% amortization for 6 years.

Say:

   Building has cash flow of $20,000 before P.M. 2nd mortgage.

Analysis: (ordinary seller's transaction)

1. Cash flow before P.M. 2nd Mtge.	$20,000
2. 6% interest & 3% amortization =	9,000
3. Net cash flow	$11,000

Operator's Proposal:

1. Cash flow before P.M. 2nd Mtge.	$20,000
2. 6% interest & "O" amortization	6,000
3. Net cash flow	$14,000

A $14,000 bottom line looks a good deal better than an $11,000 bottom line. The question is, is it better? The operator will tell you that you are taking your amortization out in cash instead of paying it in toward the mortgage. This is true as far as it goes. If we examine the $11,000 cash flow from an ordinary seller's transaction, a yield of 15% on equity will require approximately $73,000 cash. Conversely, the operator's purchase money mortgage creates a synthetic $14,000 yield and will require approximately $93,000 cash for a 15% yield on equity. By eliminating your amortization charge the operator very often is able to secure a greater price. In this particular hypothetical case, the operator would net an additional $20,000. Either stay away from operator deals or make your calculations as you would in an ordinary seller's transaction. The other method of creating a blown up yield is the use of a third mortgage. Third mortgages went out of style many years ago and really are no longer worthy of discussion.

Additional Points

We are living in an era of rising costs. These costs can, over a period of years, erode the margin of profit. We do have ways of combating this problem. We cannot create a built-in protection against all increases but we can protect against the following:

1. Increased labor costs.
2. Increased insurance cost.
3. Increased taxes.

Whenever a new lease is signed, or a lease renewed, it is mandatory that protective clauses be included in the lease protecting the landlord against increases. This is done simply by inserting a clause that it will be the tenant's obligation to assume a proportionate share of any increase of the aforementioned items. Surprisingly few tenants fight this clause.

When negotiating for an office building the owner will in many cases present you with very lean expense figures. This really is not cheating, but rather presentation of an area in which negotiation is expected. In order to have a strong position and be aware of the true cash flow, it is imperative that you do not fool yourself. Follow the guidelines, as outlined in this chapter, but do not make the expenses more than they actually are.

Exaggeration on your part is not being safe, but really being foolish. If you, as a buyer, distort the expenses, then your offer for the property will also be distorted. You may then lose a good buy, because you were overzealous in calculating the expenses. Calculate true expenses and make your offer based upon these expenses.

What To Look For

Office buildings sites. A visit to the downtown area may reveal available parcels that are vacant. Where plottage is available a broker is a must. The broker will have information that the individual would find most difficult to acquire. If there are no vacant parcels available you may still be able to secure a choice site. Invariably there are one and two-story taxpayers available. Office building sites are expensive, but often by overpaying for a taxpayer you may secure a site below market price. The only problem, all other things being equal, is to make certain that the existing tenancies have either no leases or short leases. Possession is of paramount importance.

Change of use. There are buildings available that have many vacancies, these vacancies being caused by reasons other than location. One particular building comes to mind that had a 40% vacancy factor. The problem was its outmoded layout. The building had many, many small offices and it seemed that tenants wanted larger space. The building was purchased very reasonably, renamed the "Buyers Mart," and the office space offered to the public. Within sixty days all of the small offices were leased as small buying offices. The value of an office building is best exploited by a recognition of its prime use.

10

Investing In Residential Properties

When approaching the making of money in real estate, the general public thinks that important money can only be made by influential real estate operators. Nothing could be further from the facts. Many average-income people have produced fortunes in real estate. In truth, many of them made their fortunes by accident.

Buy For The Future

When purchasing a one family dwelling it is advisable to acquire with an eye to the future. I met a man, some years ago, who had an engaging story to tell. Throughout the depression in the 30's he was unable to secure a job so he decided to use his life savings to buy a farm. He reasoned that a farm would at least give his family food to eat. This man went out to Levittown, Long Island, New York and secured a small house and plot of land that was some five acres in size. He farmed the land and succeeded in producing a living during the depression. When World War II came jobs were plentiful. The working of the farm was scaled down considerably because of lack of time, and the site was basically used as a home site.

Population Explosion—Financial Explosion

In 1946 William Leavitt decided to do something about the population explosion. Leavitt started to erect thousands of homes. These were built upon sides of a main highway, Hempstead Turnpike. The plot that cost the farmer approximately $3,500 was now rapidly increasing in value. A major oil company leased the corner parcel, comprising one acre, for $1,200 per month net. The one family residence on the property was sold for $12,000. Not bad for a man who bought a one family house with a little land for farming. However, the profit factor had not yet been completed. The remaining part, three acres, was sold for a shopping center. The price—a cool $150,000. Now, how much money was made from the sale of the property?

One family house	$ 12,000
Three acres	150,000
Gas station lease*	240,000
Total profit	$402,000

*At that time net leased gas stations were being sold to show a 6% yield on equity.

The pecuniary gain made by the farmer was 112 times the purchase price. With his profits the farmer gave half of the money to his children and moved further east to Riverhead, New York. The farmer bought another large plot for little money, in what he hoped was the path of progress. Regretably, I do not know if the farmer hit it rich again. I never saw him again. I do know that since his purchase Riverhead has expanded considerably.

The farmer was not a professional real estate man, but he was following the formula for success that sophisticated realty men follow. Buy on a main highway and wait for progress to catch up with you.

George The Millionaire

I know a chap who lives in California and is in the electronics business. I know that he had been a poor boy who never had any advantages. Today, he is a multimillionaire and heads a gigantic electronics firm. The foundation of his success was the purchase of a one family dwelling.

After the Korean War he left the Army with an honorable discharge and little else. He went to school under the G.I. Bill of Rights and studied electronics. Following that he pursued the usual path—a job, a wife and then two children. He seemed to have everything except money. It took him about five years to save up three thousand dollars, which he intended to use to purchase a house. George looked for over a year, but could not find anything he could afford. Finally, a broker showed him a house he could afford, but it had drawbacks. The house was situated in Massapequa, Long Island, New York on Merrick Road. Merrick Road is a business street and as such has a maximum of noise and obnoxious odors from the thousands of cars using it. After considerable deliberation it was decided that the house should be purchased. George reasoned that with a little work he could fence in the property and at least make it reasonably safe to raise his children. The house was purchased for thirty thousand dollars with $3,000 cash. The balance was a first mortgage.

George now had two jobs. His daytime job was for paying off the twenty-seven thousand dollar mortgage, his evening job for putting the house into shape. Throughout this period of approximately three years while George labored along, someone else was also working—builders. Several large builders had purchased land in Massapequa and were erecting hundreds of one family homes. This active building continued along at a brisk pace and the homes circled George's neighborhood. Somewhere near this time the Merrick Road property suddenly became valuable, because Merrick Road was the logical location for the erection of stores to supply the needs of the many families moving into Massapequa. George's property, which comprised slightly under three acres, was now the subject of bidding by commercial builders. I sold the property for George for $135,000. After paying off his mortgage, legal fees and brokerage commission George netted approximately $100,000. Much of the proceeds was later used to purchase a partnership in a California electronics firm.

Reflecting, one might say that the foundation of George's success was the purchase of a "poorly located," run-down one family dwelling.

At one time I owned some very old tenements that required continuous repair. I employed a young fellow named Jimmy S. He was a high school drop-out, but an energetic young man with a way with tools. Jim worked hard but never seemed to be able to get ahead. I liked him and recommended him to other property owners; still, he could not maintain himself short of just being able to survive.

Jim, The Handyman

I closed a deal and took a run-down one family dwelling in trade. I had little interest in this run-down one family house. I was hopeful of achieving a zoning change and greatly increasing the value. I thought that I had an outside opportunity of a zone change. I applied for one but unfortunately was turned down. I now owned a property for which I had absolutely no use. With its present zoning the land was worth about $2,000. However, the house would cost about $2,000 to demolish. The house itself was really in bad shape and would require about $10,000 to put it in moderate condition. I spoke to Jim, several weeks after the zoning board had turned me down, and he expressed considerable interest. He wanted to purchase the property. I wanted to get rid of the house, but I did not want to see Jim stuck. I suggested that he inspect the premises and then let me know if he still wanted to purchase the house. The next day Jim was just as eager to buy the property. I couldn't sell the property and so I decided to make a present of it to Jim.

Jim had an idea that he could do all the labor required and he was right. However, not being an experienced businessman he had not contemplated the five thousand dollars needed to purchase material. He went to a bank for a loan, but it was not forthcoming. I felt that as long as I was involved this far I would go a little further—I co-signed a $5,000 note.

Jim did a tasteful job of remodeling the house and put it up for sale. Within two weeks the house was sold for $15,000. Jim paid off the $5,000 loan and pocketed a $10,000 profit. Beginning with the $10,000 seed money Jim eventually purchased a large contracting firm. The story does not end here. Many years later I temporarily overextended myself and needed a $100,000 second mortgage. You've guessed it—I got the loan from Jim!

Have Courage—Invest

Aside from individual purchasers, real estate brokers are the largest single purchasers of one family homes. These purchases are made for two reasons: first, in order to tie up a house and thus be able to make a commission; second, because the house is a genuine buy and may be turned over for a profit. The first reason is a necessity, because there is a shortage of good resales available. The second requires skill that only an experienced home salesman may possess. The vast majority of the "buys" are houses in need of remodeling. The broker must be able to figure his cost of acquisition, cost of remodeling, sales expense and then decide if it is all worth it.

Many people have the talent to acquire excellent buys, but lack the courage to make the investment. Other people have the knowledge plus the guts to acquire good buys. All this seems to boil down to needing courage to make money in the one family field.

Plan For One Family Profits

Stories concerning people who have made considerable monies through the purchase of one family residences always delight me. Many of these lucky people have made correct investment moves by accident, and luckily have made money. Some people are not lucky, but are planners.

There are many planners who are making money with one family homes. These people seem to be all using the same formula—conversion. The procedure is basically simple. One family dwellings of eight rooms or more are purchased. The best type of neighborhood for this type of operation is a low end middle class area—just a cut above ghetto. Most of these old homes have two bathrooms, one on the first floor and one on the second floor. The first floor always contains a kitchen. A kitchen is built on the second floor. The major cost is a hot and cold water line. Knock down cabinets are relatively cheap. Then a second-hand electric stove and second-hand refrigerator are installed. The houses used for this type conversion are side hall dwellings that easily lend to the creation of two separate entrances. We now have a one family dwelling converted to a two family.

The so-called retail price for conversions is 50% over base cost. In other words a single family dwelling that has a fair market value of say $25,000 is worth $37,500 when it is converted to a two family dwelling. The cost of conversion, in most parts of the country, is approximately $3,500. The cash equity investment is generally $5,000. Consequently, the yield on cash equity is 147%. There are plenty of large, old one family homes just waiting for someone to convert them. In a number of instances housewives have been buying, remodeling and selling for profit. Profits are there for anyone who will take a little time and effort.

In purchasing residential properties, either large or small, it is mandatory to determine if there will be an effective income. Will your tenants stay? Can vacancies be quickly leased? There are a number of sources that maintain such statistics. Real Estate Boards, owners associations and local newspapers appear to be the best sources for securing this type of information.

In order to achieve the maximum benefit from a residential property it is necessary to have some imagination plus facts. The available options are many. The art of conversion appears to be the quickest path to success.

A young retail merchant known as Whitey Tunafish put together an interesting conversion. This chap was a young, blond-haired man who loved tuna fish sandwiches, consequently the strange name. Whitey purchased his building in a large eastern city known for its many colleges. A great many of the colleges had no dormitories and every year there was considerable skirmishing for the available apartments. Whitey decided to alleviate this condition and make money at the same time.

Whitey purchased an old and once luxurious office building. The layouts consisted of offices having one to four rooms. The existing layouts were not changed as this would have quickly outpriced the venture. The only changes made in the building consisted of the installation of kitchens and kitchenettes and the addition of bathrooms. The property had been purchased quite cheaply, because of the building's vacancy factor which was 25%. As existing office tenants leases expired they were not renewed. All of the leases were of short duration and did not create much of a problem. The building was not a large one containing a total of 10,000 square feet. The building was set up as follows:

Rent roll (if 100% leased)	$35,000
Operating expenses	17,500
Available for debt service	$17,500

1st mortgage of $100,000 at 8% interest and 1% amortization		9,000
Cash flow (if 100% leased)		$ 8,500
Vacancies (25%)		(8,750)
Actual negative cash flow		$(250)

The building was losing money and the owners were most anxious to get out from under. Whitey purchased the building by assuming the existing first mortgage and paid $25,000 cash over the first mortgage. The investment, of course, also involved some $60,000 in alterations. The alteration figure is low because of the building layout. Originally the building had been built as a luxurious medical building and contained many lavatories and bathrooms—these were fully utilized.

Whitey was able to secure a second mortgage in the amount of $60,000 at 12% interest and 2% amortization for a period of ten years. After the alterations and secondary financing the building set up quite differently.

(1)	Rent roll (actual)		$40,000
(2)	Expenses		15,000
	Available for debt service		$25,000
	1st mortgage, Int. and Amort.	$9,000	
	2nd mortgage, Int. and Amort.	$8,400	17,400
	Cash flow		$ 7,600
(3)	Cash over financing $35,000		
	Return on cash equity 21.7%		

Remarks:

(1) By leasing the space to students, generally four to each four room unit, the rent roll was increased to $40,000.

(2) By eliminating office cleaning, at $25,000 per annum, the expense item was cut.

(3) The cash invested was:

Original cash over financing	$25,000
Bonus and mortgage expenses	10,000
Total cash invested	$35,000

In utilizing a community need Whitey was able to create a handsome profit for himself and to also make available badly needed rental units.

The art of conversion has wide horizons. I have seen office buildings remodeled into apartments and apartments changed into office units. I have also seen apartment buildings changed into rooming houses, loft buildings changed into condominiums, and store properties changed into apartments. The basic foundation for all of these changes has always been the same—need. A prospective purchaser must do some investigative real estate study in order to determine community needs—needs that may lead to individual profits.

The purchase of a residential property may seem a bit difficult for a "non real estate" person. This is a classification that most purchasers fall into. Real estate people are not born, they come from other lines of business. It is reassuring to a prospective purchaser if he can make a reasonable appraisal that will satisfy him that he has been able to determine a proper price or that he has been able to reject an overpriced property. This can be done with a fair degree of accuracy by using the appraisal method.

The appraisal method is reasonably accurate according to the amount of homework that a prospective purchaser is willing to complete. A rough appraisal of a small residential property may be done easily and quickly.

First determine the value of the land beneath the building. This is done best by comparing prices with similar properties. In this example we will use some hypothetical figures. Let us say that we have a land value of $12,000 and a net profit, on a free and clear basis, of $4,000. Now let us proceed to the appraisal. The appraisal is done on a free and clear basis in order to keep out synthetic values created by "gimmick" financing.

(1)	Take 10% of the land value (10% is a reasonable figure)	$ 1,200
(2)	Subtract the capitalized value of the land from the net profit. $4,000 minus $1,200 =	2,800
(3)	Take 10% of the result of calculations of #2, plus a 20 year recovery (5%) $2,800 @ 15%	18,648
(4)	Land value	12,000
	Total value	$34,648

Note: Where comparable properties show more or less
returns this #3 factor should be adjusted.

The previous example is not to be construed as true and exact value. In the hands of a layman it can only be a guide and should be accepted as such.

A small investor may bring about personal satisfaction from ownership of a residential property. There are a number of unusual types of property that are available even to the small investor. An acquaintance of mine, actually my neighborhood druggist, purchased an interesting property. The building that he acquired was an old cottage containing some twenty rooms. The building was remodeled into twelve 1½ room units plus a lobby and a tenant recreation room.

Now, the large problem appeared to be the leasing of the apartments. The immediate area was unsatisfactory, containing relatively numerous small homes and a quantity of ancient apartment dwellings. The people who dwell in this community do so for the reason that the rentals are low. On the credit side the location was close to transportation facilities, both bus and subway being available and furnishing excellent transportation to all parts of the city. The druggist came up with a novel idea—he advertised the apartment units for young singles only. No married couples need apply. Within ten days the apartments were 100% leased. The young people loved living there. They also liked the parties, arranged on a monthly basis by the landlord, in the community recreation room.

The druggist is delighted with his building and the tenants are rather fond of their landlord. In fact, the tenants held an appreciation party for the landlord, just a short while back. An added feature, of which the landlord is quite proud, is the six marriages between tenants that have taken place during the past six years.

What To Look For

Residential properties may generally be divided into three categories—new, old and unimproved. Each is a separate entity and requires a separate look.

Unimproved property offers the investor two choices. First, he may purchase a plot at the market value. Secondly he may look for an opportunity that offers a chance to make a substantial profit. In order to achieve this profit it is necessary to purchase a cheap, unimproved parcel, wait several years and then cash in. How is this done? The answer is by looking, looking for a parcel that is out of the high priced land district, but in the path of progressive expansion.

Dealing with improved properties is slightly more complicated. New buildings are generally the highest and best use for the land they set upon. If the building is successful you can secure the normal market yield. This yield, while not bad, is not a bonanza.

In order to achieve a big bonanza it is necessary to work with older residential properties. If the property is in trouble and can be purchased cheaply then you must look for the change possibility. These possibilities are:

> Rooming House
> Changing large units to smaller units
> Offices
> Cooperatives
> Condominiums
> Single Tenancy

If the change appears feasible, make it and you will make money.

11

Leaseholds—An Untapped Source of Wealth

Real estate is, contrary to Wall Street doctrines, a predictable, mature industry. Real estate has far surpassed the stodgy Wall Street security business. Real estate lobbies have secured tax advantages. Real estate builders and investors have worked out ingenious creations in order to further the industry. One of the innovations created is the leasehold. Personally, I have an affection for leaseholds because of their brilliancy and sheer simplicity.

The significance of the leasehold is clearly evident when we grasp that any type of real estate may be included in a leasehold transaction. This would apply to both improved or unimproved property. Because of its many variations and possibilities the leasehold is the king of real estate.

One of the prominent features of the leasehold arrangement is the savings involved in land purchase. A client of mine owned a 100' x 100' parcel which he had been trying to sell for over two years without receiving a single offer. There was a "for sale" sign on the property but all it did was evoke a few telephone calls. Nothing came of these calls. My office secured a tenant who was interested in leasing if the owner would erect a building. The owner of the land, a Mr. Wilson, did not have the money to erect a building. If we did not produce a deal there was a strong possibility that Mr. Wilson might lose his land for nonpayment of taxes.

Something had to be done and done quickly in order to save Mr. Wilson's property. Without money to build a building and inability to hold the property, the problem appeared insurmountable.

As vacant land the property appeared to hold no interest for prospective purchasers. I then decided to attack the problem as improved property. First, I offered the property on a "build to suit" basis. Nothing happened. I then submitted the proposition to fixture people in diverse lines of occupations. The fixture people are considerable aids to both builders and brokers. The fixture people are naturally interested in selling fixtures and so they are always willing to submit a good location to their clients. What actually happens is that an unusually large group of people going into business for the first time are interested in knowing what opening a retail store will cost. In this manner the fixture people obtain new customer leads. Established business people also come to their favorite fixture firm, because they are satisfied with both fixtures and financing—or both.

My fishing expedition proved successful. A dry cleaning fixture company produced a dry cleaner who was interested in paying $15,000 per annum with a 100% tax stop. The cleaner required a 3,000 square foot building that would cost approximately $45,000. I now had the foundation upon which to construct a deal.

I knew that the vacant land was of little interest to possible purchasers. I decided to make the vacant land more attractive. I offered the property for sale as a land lease. The property was to be sold with a land lease of $2,500 per annum, and with the land owners interest subordinated to an institutional first mortgage to be placed on a building to be erected. On these terms the property was conveyed for $25,000. We now had some money to work with.

My immediate move was to arrange for a first mortgage. The bank wanted to see a proposed profit and loss statement. I made up the following estimate:

Gross Rental:		$15,000
Estimated Expenses:		
Taxes (100% stop)	$2,100	
Insurance	500	
Repairs	200	
Land Lease Rent	2,500	$ 5,300
Cash Flow, Free & Clear		$ 9,700

I was able to secure a $45,000 first mortgage at 8% interest and 2% amortization for fifteen years. The net profit setup appeared as follows:

Cash Flow Free and Clear	$9,700
Interest and amortization 1st mortgage	4,500
	$5,200

Mr. Wilson advised me that he was going to retire and live in Florida. Could I sell the building for him? Of course. The deal was clear and had a 100% tax stop. I offered the deal about and had several offers. The best offer was $52,000 cash over the first mortgage.

How did Wilson make out? Let us analyze the entire deal.

Expenses:		
	Estimated value of land	$ 25,000
	Cost of building	45,000
	Brokerage commissions	11,000
	Total cost to Wilson	$ 81,000
Income		
	Sale of Land Lease	$ 25,000
	1st mortgage funds	45,000
	Sale of leasehold	52,000
		$122,000
	Total expense	81,000
	Total profit	$ 41,000

It assuredly took a lot of doing, but because of a leasehold arrangement we were able to get $41,000 profit for a $25,000 property—a parcel that had stood for two years without any interest being shown in the property. Possibly, even the asking price of $25,000 for the land was inflated.

Leasehold Is The Builder's Friend

A man, who today is a multimillionaire builder, told me an interesting story concerning leaseholds. During the Great Depression he wanted to build, but had no money. This did not stop him. The builder, known to his friends as Big Tom, vaulted the first hurdle by making a land conveying arrangement. The proprietor of the land consented to a long duration lease on his land and to subordinate to an institutional first mortgage. Big Tom had an inclination to make use of the property with a small garden apartment of thirty families.

When the scheme was offered to the bank that was to furnish the temporary and permanent financing, they showed considerable uneasiness. The bank was of the opinion that a thirty family job might be too much for the area. Big Tom used his most convincing manner and persuaded a reluctant bank to agree to financing a thirty family garden apartment building.

Big Tom continued, "I got the loan against the bank's advice." Then he stopped talking—for a moment there was silence. I asked, "What happened, Tom?" "The bank was right, I went broke," he replied. There is a moral to this story. A leasehold is a marvelous tool with which to work. In many cases it is a remedy to relieve a lack of financing. But even a leasehold can become unpleasant if improperly used. In Big Tom's situation this was an important monetary lesson and through the appropriate use of the leasehold he went on to an extremely successful career as a builder.

Certain people might think that a leasehold is a tool used by a financial finagler or a sophisticated sharpie. Nothing could be further from the truth. The real estate profession is no different from other lines of business. Both builders and investors sometimes need a little more help than a lending institution can provide. Leaseholds supply this help.

Leaseholds Also Help Investors

The leasehold is a generous help to investors from every walk of life. Doctors, lawyers, butchers, dentists, plumbers—all are investors and all can use the aid that leaseholds provide. The leasehold has helped many nonprofessional real estate people achieve financial security. The leasehold has helped many a family pay for their children's college education.

The leasehold has many advantages. There generally are two parts to the leasehold. First, is the owner of the fee—the land, and the second is the leasehold improvement. The ownership of improved property on leased land has a definite tax advantage. Ordinarily, the land under an improvement cannot be depreciated, but the improvement itself may be depreciated. Let us assume a building is purchased for $100,000 and the land beneath the building is valued at $25,000. The government will permit depreciation of the value difference between land and building, provided that the difference is in favor of the building. In the situation under discussion $75,000, or 75% of the transaction, can be depreciated.

Now, let us assume that we have a leasehold transaction. Let us say that a building is purchased for $100,000 on leased land. In this situation the government permits depreciation of the entire purchase price. The leasehold is a variable tool. Breaking it all down to dollars we have the following figures:

Assumption: 3% depreciation rate

Leasehold purchase	Outright sale
$100,000	$ 75,000
3%	3%
$ 3,000 may be depreciated	$ 2,250 may be depreciated

Over the years the leasehold has been accepted as one of the more sophisticated realty tools.

Know Your Leasehold And Its Advantages

Numerous investors are wary of leaseholds because they feel the need to actually own something. Somehow this reasoning sounds more superior than it is. First, land leases run for a period of between 60 and 99 years. This is a considerable time. Over this duration better than average yields are available. Leaseholds historically show better yields than fully deeded properties. Taxwise, leaseholds are shown greater preference by the government. It should be remembered, however, that as the initial lessee, you may subject the terms of the leasehold to negotiation. The most important business aspects of the lease are the following:

> Length of Lease
> Refinancing Terms
> Restrictions
> Financing Restrictions
> Options & Increases
> Rent

Inspecting the leasehold from the other side of the fence we run into a different situation. The owner of a prime parcel of land may not be interested in selling for many reasons. Some of the reasons are:

Property has been in family many years
Cannot sell because of tax situation
Several owners who cannot agree upon a sale
Owners seeking income rather than capital gains

The number of owners who prefer to lease is large and it helps to make potential leasehold deals available. It may require a little patience, but the leasehold deal that is suitable for an individual investor can be achieved without too much trouble. An item that also has greatly helped the surge of leasehold deals is the inflated price of land. Some investors now prefer to lease rather than buy.

What To Look For

Leaseholds may be real estate's greatest contribution to investors. The different variations are almost infinite. If you want to get into realty investing and are short on cash but long on effort, leaseholds may be your entrance.

Throughout the country there are many mismanaged properties. The owners of these properties are either breaking even or possibly losing money. Look for these properties. With proper application and expert brokerage advice wonders can be worked and monies made.

Another type of property that is available to the leasehold broker is the successful property, one that is making money. Leasing a property offers advantages to the lessor. Suppose a building contains 60 tenants; by leasing the property the owner now has only one tenant to deal with and removes himself from the problems of management. For the lessee there is an opportunity—the opportunity to take over a building and pocket increases in revenue that he can achieve. The leasehold rental is ordinarily 3% less than the cash flow. In some instances the lessor maintains 50% of any rental increases. The lessor is now free of management, participates in rental increases and retains all amortization.

It is sometimes a little difficult to obtain a leasehold deal but with persistence it can be done. In order to make a deal it may be necessary to sweeten the deal by posting security with the lessor. This will greatly aid in cementing a deal.

12

Reaping Big Profits From Cooperative Apartments

While the co-operative apartment has been with us for a number of years, relatively speaking, it has only lately come under the microscope of comparison. The recent extraordinary growth of the condominiums has brought the two types of property ownership into direct comparison.

The co-op is actually individual or corporate ownership of shares in a corporation. The corporation in most instances will own an apartment building. I say "most instances" because there are co-ops that own office buildings, shopping centers, marinas and golf clubs. The co-op owner in the apartment building is a stockholder with a proprietary lease.

Co-ops have had a solid rise over many years.

Their sales have increased steadily since 1946. Three reasons for this success have been financing, tax credits, and equity build-up.

The financing of cooperative apartments is both easy and immediate. Savings banks today are offering 75%, 20-year mortgages. The banks are so desirous of getting these loans that they are advertising and even have application forms printed in newspapers. In addition, sponsors of co-ops are lending 25% to prospective purchasers. Consequently no down payments are necessary.

An additional advantage to co-op owning is the tax and equity advantages. These advantages include interest charges on mortgages, depreciation for maintenance and depreciation of overall property. The equity build-up, of course, has a decided advantage over a dresser-drawer full of rent receipts.

Prompt sale has been another desired end to co-op owning. The history of co-op sales has been very successful, that is, except for 1969. During this period co-ops fell upon bad times as prices dropped. The type affected most severly was the luxury market which dropped and stabilized at 33% below its 1969 high.

An engaging sidelight is the recent auction sales method of selling co-ops. There is a fee of $250 charged for listing the property. If the property is sold a commission of 3½% is charged for prices up to $75,000. Prices over $75,000 command a commission of 2½%. The seller may, if he is not satisfied with the last bid, buy back his own apartment. The only people unhappy about the co-op auctions are the real estate brokers; the co-op auction commission rates are lower than those charged by brokers.

Cooperative Financing

One item of interest in comparing co-ops against condominiums is the mortgage situation. The co-op has the advantage. Condominium mortgages are issued to individuals. Co-op mortgages are issued to the co-op corporation. Generally the co-op corporation is considerably stronger financially than any individual purchasing a condominium. Consequently the co-ops achieve better financing. It might also be added that condominium owners pay legal and mortgage expenses to acquire title to their apartments. There is no direct charge for legal or mortgage expenses to the co-op purchaser.

I have been acquainted with any number of co-op operators. These are people who make it their business to acquire older, luxury-type properties, rehabilitate and in general salvage the property. Operators make their profit by converting buildings into co-ops.

Co-op operators have, in recent years, been referred to as unscrupulous operators. The charge is false, except for a small minority —who make the headlines. As in any business there are "bad apples" in co-op operating. The deeds of these marginal operators are blown up and misrepresented to include all operators. Possibly the best way to do away with these people is to expose their methods.

The owner of a co-op apartment believes that the tenants in his building, through their board of directors, control the operation of the property. Not necessarily so. Not all co-ops are completely sold out. Many only have 35-40% of their apartments sold. In a situation like this the operators retain enough votes to operate the property as they see fit because they control 60-65% of the votes. In effect the property would be controlled by people who do not live in the building.

Beware Of Marginal Operators

If the co-op operator is legitimate there is no problem. However, the marginal operator causes many problems. If this operator fails to meet his mortgage payments the other co-op owners may be placed in a financial bind, or even lose title to their apartments.

Once again, if the marginal operator owns a majority of the stock he may "extra" the tenants to death. There can be extra charges for parking, swim clubs, laundry rooms, etc. There may also be extra heavy management fees. I know of one situation where the management firm charged 15% profit for all repairs made. This charge was in addition to the management fee.

The problem of outside ownership is a knotty one that exists primarily where a majority of the apartments have not been sold. This situation enables the majority interest to control the price of apartments and to greatly benefit themselves. It also enables the majority to control the type of tenancy.

I recollect a group of people contemplating involvement in building a co-op. They came to my office seeking to obtain investment-counseling advice. The first thing to settle was a mode of procedure. A corporation was to be formed whose function was to erect a building, sell shares of stock which entitled the shareholder to a proprietary lease covering a designated apartment, and to operate the building. It was further decided that this property would be a middle income co-op. Middle income was chosen over the other two types, luxury and low-income.

Title 213 Financing

In order to secure foremost financing it was decided to avail the corporation of Title 213 financing. The original concept of Title 213 was to aid non-profit co-ops through Federal mortgage guarantees. However, it is possible for builders and sponsors to participate in this program.

It was further decided·to erect a new building rather than convert an older building. Erecting a new building would provide greater avenues for sponsor profit. If an older building was purchased it would require great cash outlays. Situations requiring cash would be:

1. Cash over financing (about 25% of purchase price).
2. Purchasing leases of tenants who refuse to buy or move. (This is optional.)
3. Remodeling building to attract purchasers. (About 20% of purchase price in older buildings.)
4. Commissions, advertising, legal fees can run to 20% of the purchase price.

The various expenses would ascend to a consideration of 65% over the original cost. We felt that this was prohibitive. A procedure was required to invest less and make more. The answer: land lease.

The land lease afforded the opportunity for the developers to avoid investing substantial amounts of money. Ordinarily, the rule of thumb provides for 75% financing which covers the price of the building, while the remaining 25% covers the cost of land acquisition. With a land lease the sponsors were able to save the 25% land cost and were only obligated to a land rental of $20,000 per annum. The $20,000 land rental became a fixed expense and was a regular maintenance charge borne by the tenants.

While the tenants had a fixed land rent expense they also had a greater depreciation base in that the entire cost of the project could be used for depreciation calculations; land not being depreciable is deducted in fee situations.

The total cost of the job was $750,000. It would have been $1,000,000 if the land purchase had been necessary. The tenants were able to purchase their apartments at a lower figure. The sponsor still was able to get an attractive price for the apartments and cleared a $150,000 profit. This was without actually having any equity money in the job. Some front money was used, but this was recaptured through the financing.

It has been determined that one of the advantages of sponsoring a co-op as against an apartment building is in the sales value of co-ops. A co-op unit will ordinarily bring a price of 12-15% greater than the over-all sale of an apartment building.

Co-ops are supposedly running in direct competition with condominiums. Actually there will be no winners or losers. There are those who will purchase co-op apartments and there are those who will yearn for a nice condominium.

Advantages of Co-op Owning

In my opinion the co-op has enjoyed success in this country because of a number of advantages that are offered. The purchaser enjoys tax advantages in that taxes, interest and depreciation are given favorable governmental treatment. Builders are able to secure F.H.A. mortgages that enable them to completely mortgage out. Owners of existing buildings are partial to conversions because they achieve a better price for their buildings. The tenants, on the other hand, gain the benefit of lower carrying charges. The purchasers of new cooperatives also have an incentive, the provocative incentive being the ability to secure second mortgage financing on their apartments. The existence of the second mortgage creates a very low down payment, much lower than even those available for some single family dwellings. Any discussion of co-ops would be incomplete without remarking that the co-op is no longer as popular as it once was because of the tremendous growth of the condominium within the past few years. The condominium appears to have caught the public's fancy.

What To Look For

Many co-ops are made not born. While it is true that a large number of new co-ops are constructed, an even greater number are conversions. It is these conversions that, to a major degree, are created by operators. In order to achieve success the operators follow set formulas.

Building type. It should be the older, gracious type of apartment building. The neighborhood should be good. The key word is quality —quality of building and neighborhood. The building should be a doorman type with large lobby and other luxurious appointments.

Tenancy. The tenancy should contain middle aged to older type tenancy. The income strata should be middle to upper class.

The next step is of prime importance. A question must be answered. Do the tenants want to convert to a co-op? The usual procedure is to interview as many tenants as possible in order to learn their views. If the project appears promising an option should be secured. The option price should be negotiated in order to keep it at a minimum. At this point all tenants are contacted and if the project still seems promising then a contract is called for.

In short, look for the co-op formula and proceed along these lines. The conversion process can be quite profitable.

13

Money Making Secrets For Investing In Sandwich Leases

Today, at one time or another, we hear talk about being without frontiers to conquer. Gone are the ancient cries of "Go West, young man." Really, it is not necessary to go anyplace, merely to stay where you are. What happens if you stay put? You can influence the opportunities that surround you.

Big Money Not Necessary; Nor Travel

Even though you do not have a substantial amount of money, you may still become a substantial real estate operator, in some instances without any money whatsoever. It should be remembered that these almost unbelievable opportunities are probably available in every town or hamlet in the United States. So don't think you need move in many directions to find opportunity. Wealth and opportunity are under your very nose. Learn how to reach out for potential wealth.

What is A Sandwich Lease?

The sandwich lease or sandwich lease option is a special technique, little known, but very effective. This technical skill is so called because it involves a third party sandwiched in between the landlord and tenant. The benefit of this system is in its adaptability to both choice properties and marginal buildings. This system may be effective with buildings containing unfavorable leases and also with properties containing poor economic structuring.

The sandwich lease is used in situations where the present owner feels that there is little he can do to improve his property because of inferior leases or perhaps even a lack of money. I believe that the most suitable way to illustrate the procedure and use of the sandwich lease is to narrate several situations that I am familiar with.

An interesting pattern was expressed in a building proposed for sale last year. Details are as follows:

Gross rental:		$120,000
Expenses:		
Management	by owner	
Interest & amortization	$45,000	
Other expenses	65,000	$110,000
Cash Flow		$ 10,000

Price: $100,000 cash over financing

The property under discussion was a one story taxpayer containing a supermarket of 18,000 square feet plus five service stores containing 5,000 square feet. At one time the stores had been very much underrented and as a consequence the present owner could not find a mode to create a more desirable yield. A lot of time and effort was spent to upgrade the property, but to no advantage. Money was an urgent need and the owner did not have available funds. The property had been acquired for $100,000 cash over financing to show a 12% yield on equity ($12,000 cash flow). The present owner wanted to acquire his money back and was presenting the property for sale at $100,000. However, the income had diminished to the point where the $100,000 would only display a yield of 10% on equity. After a 3% management fee ($3,600) the effective cash flow actually was $6,400 or 6.4% yield on equity. This yield proved to be unattractive to prospective purchasers. And well it should have been. On a comparative basis single tenant AAA-1, long term leases were available to show greater yields. Many investors realize that a AAA-1 leased property is generally held in greater esteem in many respects to a taxpayer property. Superior, that is, in all respects except the opportunity to improve the financial yield of the property. It follows that there is substantially more work to manage a taxpayer than to operate an AAA-1 net net net leased property.

One of the possible purchasers interested in acquisition rejected the idea of purchasing the property for $100,000. He did, however, come up with an alternate suggestion. Would the owner be interested in participating in a sandwich lease? Possibly, if the conditions with regard to payment were attractive. After some discussion and settlement of terms it was agreed as follows:

Sandwich Lease Stipulations

(1) The lessor was to receive a net net rental of $12,000 per annum. The lease to run for a period of fifty years.

(2) The lessee shall have the right to refinance at any time. Any increase in the existing mortgage shall be divided equally between the lessor and lessee.

(3) Lessee shall have the option, at any time after the tenth year, to purchase the property. The purchase price shall be cash over the existing financing to give a 10% yield on equity. In no event shall the purchase price be less than $100,000 cash over financing.

(4) The lessee agrees to pay, for the lease position, the sum of $20,000 to the lessor.

The owner was able to lease his property and the lessee was also highly pleased with the deal. The initial move by the lessee was to contact the bank holding the mortgage with a request to refinance in the same amount as the existing balance. The original mortgage had been for $400,000 with 8% interest and the balance as amortization. The total yearly payment was $45,000. The mortgage was recast in the amount of the then existing balance of $300,000, at 10% interest and 2% amortization. The yearly cost now became $36,500. The recasting of the mortgage answered the purpose of increasing the

bank's interest yield by 2%, but it also increased the cash flow by
$8,500 per annum. With this extraordinary great increase in cash
flow, lessee now had funds with which to improve the building and
the expectation of obtaining superior tenants at increased rentals.

Problem Properties—Sandwich Candidates

A different deal implicating a sandwich was consummated some
years ago and thereby we were granted the opportunity of investigating the outcome in considerable degree. The property under
examination was a one story supermarket rented on a gross lease.
The building primarily was constructed with expectations of renting
to an aggregate of tenants. There was a difficulty in leasing and in
desperation the building was leased to a single tenant, a supermarket.
In lieu of the expectation of $4.00 per square foot net, the property
had been leased for $2.50 gross. The area of the market was 10,000
square feet. Moreover, because the tenant was not rated, the
financing was not sufficient. At this particular period the owner
entered into a sandwich lease option. The tenant had previously used
ten years of an original fifteen year lease. The financial organization
was set up as follows:

Gross rental:		$25,000
Expenses:		
Taxes	$ 8,000	
Maintenance	1,500	
Repairs	1,500	
Insurance	2,500	
Interest & amortization	10,000	
Other	$ 1,000	$24,500
Cash Flow		$ 500

The Sandwich Gamble

The owner's cash flow was a meager $500 a year. In the ordinary
condition of events this type of cash flow, at this period, was worth
perhaps $4,000 cash over financing. A prospect appeared who was
interested in a sandwich lease option. This prospect proposed to pay
$25,000 per annum for the market lease, on a net basis, all expenses
except the mortgage to be paid by the lessee. The sandwich lease
created a drastic change in the lessor's position.

Lessor Position

Net rental	$25,000
Mortgage expense	10,000
Cash flow to lessor	$15,000

Lessee Position

Net rental	$25,000
Expenses (less mortgage)	14,500
Cost to lessee	($39,500)

The cost to the lessee, including rent and expenses, was $39,500. The gross rental received was $25,000. Consequently, the yearly loss proved to be $14,500. Compounded over the next five years the loss to the lessee would be $72,500. The lessee anticipated this future loss and was disposed to take it for he felt the locality was increasing in influence and at the end of five years he anticipated an opportunity to retake his investment plus a suitable pecuniary gain.

Conditions of Sandwich Lease Option

(a) The lessee had the option to purchase at a 12% yield, on a free and clear basis, anytime after the fifth year.

(b) The lessee had the right to lease after the expiration of the present lease to the present or to a designated new tenant.

(c) Lessee had the right to recover any money consumed rehabilitating the property by deducting same from purchase price.

(d) Any increase in financing over $100,000 was to be divided equally between lessor and lessee.

(e) Security in the amount of $25,000 was to be deposited with the lessor. Interest was to be paid annually at going certificate of deposit rates. At the expiration of the lease or in the event of a bonafide sale said security was to be refunded to lessee.

(f) Lease was to run for a period of 25 years, plus one five year option providing for a cost of living increase.

The Progress of a Sandwich Lease Option

Five years went by and the original supermarket tenant's lease expired. A chain supermarket was secured at a rental of $25,000 per annum net net net against 1½% of gross earnings. At this position the holder of the sandwich lease (lessee) was breaking even—that is, aside from the possibility of accomplishing additional surplus from the overage portion of the lease.

With the upward inflationary trend, increase in local population and the general expertise of the supermarket chain the overages were excellent. For the first two years the market averaged $3,000,000 per annum gross business; for the next two years the average sales were $4,000,000.

During this five year period the lessee produced his first money. The schedule of profit follows:

1st year	$ 45,000
2nd year	45,000
3rd year	45,000
4th year	60,000
5th year	60,000

$255,000 represents profit for 6 to 10 years.
 197,500 represents loss for 1 to 5 years.
$ 57,500 10 year rental profit

Next, the taxpayer was refinanced. After some negotiating and shopping about, a mortgage was secured in the amount of $300,000 at 8% interest and 2% amortization. The total yearly interest and amortization cost was $30,000. Subtracted from the net rental of $60,000 we obviously created a net cash flow of $30,000.

The lessee decided to exercise his option to purchase, which according to the terms of the sandwich lease was at 12% equity on a free and clear basis. The purchase price was $500,000. The lessee without delay turned his contract over for $600,000. The new purchaser achieved a good buy at being able to secure a 10% net net net lease.

Adding Up the Lessee's Profits

After all of this maneuvering, allow me to show just what occurred. The recent mortgage was for $300,000. The lessee received 50% of all funds over $100,000. This gave the lessee a mortgage profit of $100,000 plus his rental profit of $57,500 or a total of $157,500. Another $100,000 was acquired on the sale of the contract. For the ten years of ownership the lessee averaged $25,750 per annum. Not bad for an individual who invested nothing (although he did put up $25,000 in security). We must then conclude that the lessee did quite well with no actual cash investment.

How Well Did the Lessor Do?

How well did the lessor do? Let us determine the change, if any, in his equity position. At the time that the sandwich lease was entered into the cash value, or equity position, was valued at approximately $4,000. After the sandwich lease was closed the lessor's position immediately improved in that his cash flow showed an instant increase to $15,000. At the market value a net cash flow of $15,000 had a value of about $125,000. I defy anyone to show me another business where a man can sell a marginal situation for a fantastic profit, while the purchaser also makes another fantastic profit, then sells his interest to an investor who also has a good return on his money. The sandwich lease is unique in that it can make instant rich men.

The lessor's profit did not cease with the $15,000 cash flow. In the ten years that the lessee managed the property the landlord made a profit of $150,000. Again, the money continued to come in. The deluge of wealth did not stop.

The property was refinanced by the lessee according to the sandwich lease agreement, which was a 50%—50% split of all monies over $100,000. The overage was $200,000. Consequently, this provided another $100,000 for the lessor. Again, the flow of money continued. There was still more to be made.

The sale of the property by the lessee produced additional monies for the lessor. The sandwich agreement called for an option to purchase at 12% yield on equity. The option was exercised at a price of $500,000, or $200,000 over the existing mortgage. The lessor now had another $200,000.

A careful recapitulation of the profits to the lessor is as follows:

$150,000	operating profit for 10 years
100,000	mortgage profit
200,000	profit on sale
$450,000	total profit

I seriously doubt if Wall Street or any other investment source can match the opportunities possible, and the creations of wealth that only a sandwich lease may provide.

What To Look For

The sandwich lease is another of those little known operations used by sophisticated real estate men. This does not, however, prohibit the so called "non-sophisticate" or even part-time investor from utilizing the system.

The trick, of course, is to look for and seek out an ideal situation. When the proper set of circumstances is found it greatly aids in setting up a sandwich situation. Sandwich deals are rarely ever offered; generally they must be created.

In seeking a potential sandwich lease you should locate one or more of the following:

> Landlord short of ready cash
> Underrented properties
> Properties having refinancing possibilities

When a prospective parcel is located, a careful check of the surrounding area must be made in order to determine the validity of your judgment. Additional surveys must be made regarding refinancing and leasing possibilities. This information may be acquired through your own efforts and, further, through consultation with real estate investment brokers and realty consultants. This type of investigation should produce positive results. After digesting all of the facts obtained you should easily determine the feasibility of the project.

14

Five Ways To Build A Secure, Long Term Investment With "Taxpayer" Properties

Taxpayers provide the opportunity for the unsophisticated investor to get his feet wet in real estate. There are all sizes of taxpayers, of course, but I am at this time concerned with taxpayers in the $25,000 to $75,000 cash range. Basically, these properties contain a major tenant or draw, and three to five minor, service-type tenants. Once the taxpayer becomes large, say 10 to 12 or more stores, it in effect may be treated as a small, strip shopping center. In this chapter, we are concerned strictly with taxpayers.

A Taxpayer Is Not A Taxpayer

The term taxpayer is a misnomer. Many years ago, it was the custom to build a small building on a commercial parcel in order to achieve enough revenue to pay the taxes until such a time as the owner might utilize the land according to its highest and best use. Today, a taxpayer is no longer a stop-gap, but rather an ultimate investment. Rentals charged are ample to amortize land, building and to also leave a reasonable profit.

Following you will note a taxpayer listing, Illustration 13-1. I will go through a complete breakdown of this property including expenses, rental and financing. I will further discuss possible problems that may arise. I feel that this chapter is of particular importance, because it may be crucial for the small commercial investor. The taxpayer does not require any exceptional expertise, but there is room for substantial error. I believe these potential errors may be eliminated through prior knowledge.

Illustration #13-1

TAXPAYER FOR SALE
LONG TERM FINANCING
GOOD TENANCY

LOCATION:	1200 Broadway, El Centro, Calif.
PLOT SIZE:	200' x 200': Building 200' x 100' irregular, 100' x 100' and 100' x 70'
DESCRIPTION:	One story taxpayer, cement block, full basements, individual heating units. Parking at rear for 35 cars. Corner parcel.
TENANCY:	Chain Supermarket plus five individual stores.
1st MORTGAGE:	$220,000. Payable $5,500 quarterly including 8% interest and 2% amortization. Due 15 years.
ESTIMATED INCOME:	$55,000

ESTIMATED
EXPENSES:

Int. & amtz. 1st Mtge.	$22,000	
Real estate taxes	7,500	
Water	300	
Insurance	700	
Repairs	1,000	$31,500

NET RETURN: $23,500

PRICE: $470,000 with $55,000 cash balance terms.

TENANCY	SIZE	LEASE EXPIRATION	RENTAL
AAA-1 Supermarket	100' x 100'	12 years*	$30,000 per annum
Dry Cleaner	20' x 70'	7 years**	$ 5,000 per annum
Luncheonette	20' x 70'	7 years**	$ 5,000 per annum
Baker	20' x 70'	2 years**	$ 5,000 per annum
Laundromat	20' x 70'	7 years**	$ 5,000 per annum
Drug Store	20' x 70'	5 years**	$ 5,000 per annum
	17,000 sq. ft.		$55,000 per annum

*Plus 5-year option at $33,000 then additional 5-year option at $36,000.
**5-year option at $6,500.
Note: Each tenant has posted two months' security, except for the supermarket.
Subject to error, omission, prior sale or withdrawal. All without notice.

Illustration 13-1 is a typical moderate investor's deal. The first three lines in this illustration are lead lines. The owner, or broker, is attempting to tell a long story in eight words. This is typical of most listings in that the real estate industry has adopted a sort of Western Union shorthand. Basically, this is done because most sellers of real estate are of the opinion that a lengthy, detailed listing may lose the interest of the investor. I concur with this thought. Sometimes the "shorthand" is expanded into an error of omission. Legitimate expenses are not included in the listing. This must be watched for and avoided.

There is one other line that I think should be examined. At the bottom of all listings we find the following:

"Subject to error, omission, prior sale or withdrawal.
All without notice."

Listings Subject To Conditions

The sentence "Subject to error, etc.," was originally included at the bottom of all listings by real estate brokers. This was in order to protect themselves against any lawsuits that might arise because of intentional or unintentional misrepresentations by owners. Soon owners used this phrase when offering properties as principals. The phrase then degenerated as an out for some marginal brokers and owners. Carefully follow my outline for dissecting a listing and you should avoid any major problems.

Taxpayers Should Be Rated

Location for a taxpayer is a reasonably static condition. If the location is good when you purchase the property, it will in all likelihood remain good for many years. There are only two influences that can change this situation. The first is a change in the neighborhood. I refer specifically to a change where a residential community slowly goes through a metamorphosis, changing from residential to industrial. This is not an everyday occurrence, but it does happen. The initial signs are changes of zoning in the particular area. Once the municipal authorities feel that an area is going downhill, they may downgrade the zoning in an effort to bring the neighborhood back to where it may again become prosperous and in turn be able to pay taxes based on a maximum assessment. This is a process of evolution taking 15-20 years. Plenty of time, yes, but not if you come into the picture toward the cycle's end. Be sure the property is backed by solid residential properties.

The other influence that may affect a property is overbuilding. Check available land to determine how much is available within a two-mile radius that is zoned business. Some of this land will, of course, be built and provide direct competition. How your property reacts will depend upon the individual strength of your taxpayer. A taxpayer's strength is determined by its average rental per front foot. Taxpayer ratings are as follows:

Main Street Shopping	90% to 100% area	$1500 F.F. and up
Secondary Main Street	75% to 89% area	$ 800 F.F. to $1499 F.F.
Prime Neighborhood	60% to 74% area	$ 500 F.F. to $ 799 F.F.
Good Neighborhood	45% to 59% area	$ 250 F.F. to $ 499 F.F.
Weak Neighborhood	30% to 44% area	$ 215 F.F. to $ 249 F.F.
Poor Neighborhood	29% and less	$ 214 F.F. and less

Avoid the poor and weak neighborhood properties as they contain high risk factors.

Plot size for this corner parcel is 200' deep, which is good. A 100' depth does not provide for adequate parking. The building contains 17,000 square feet. Our calculations are as follows:

Total plot:	40,000 sq. ft.
Bldg. size:	17,000 sq. ft.
For parking	23,000 sq. ft.
Delivery Driveway	
(200' x 10')	2,000 sq. ft.
Net Parking	21,000 sq. ft.

We arrive at 21,000 net square feet available for parking. The generally accepted rule of thumb used in determining parking is three cars for 1,000 square feet. We can then conclude that we have approximately 60-car parking. This is quite good for a small taxpayer.

Taxpayer—The Uncomplicated One

Description of the taxpayer is uncomplicated, because the one story taxpayer is a simple four wall building. There is nothing structurally difficult or ornate about these buildings. Actually, there is far more detail to the erection of a one family dwelling. The only items we need be concerned with is the roof, basement, plumbing and sometimes the heating units. I qualified heating units because in most taxpayers of this type, each individual tenant is responsible for fuel, maintenance and repair of his own heating unit. Buildings that supply heat to tenants are considered outmoded and consequently bring much lower prices when offered for sale. Plumbing consists of one lavatory containing a bowl and sink. The exceptions to this would be luncheonettes, supermarkets, laundromats—or those lines of business that use much water. Tenants in these categories have clauses in their leases making them completely responsible for their own plumbing. In addition, they pay for the water that they use. The roof can be physically examined by actually going up on the roof or by checking the individual ceilings in each store for leaks.

The basement must be checked for a water condition. The merchants use the basements for storage of stock and so the basement is important to them. Check the basement floor and the foundation walls. Sniffing the air will reveal if a damp condition exists. A wet basement is often difficult and expensive to cure. Avoid buildings with wet basements.

Do You Have Rated Tenancy?

Tenancy in this building is according to the classic requirements. 50% of the occupancy is a good draw and also an AAA-1 tenancy. The balance of the tenancy is good service type retail establishments. The supermarket, the AAA-1 rental, pays $30,000 per annum. Even with a purchase money mortgage added to the expenses, the AAA-1 income will pay for 66% of the expenses. This is the owner's safety valve.

Can It Be Financed?

The first mortgage is a new mortgage in the amount of $220,000 at 8% interest and 2% amortization; the loan can be fully paid off in 20 years. However, this loan runs for 20 years, thus leaving a balloon. In 15 years 57.7% or $126,940 of the loan will be amortized. The balloon will thus be, rounded, $93,000. Later on in this chapter you will note that we have proposed additional financing in the amount of a $175,000 purchase money mortgage. The P.M. mortgage is at 8% constant, or 6% interest and 2% amortization. The P.M. mortgage runs for 10 years and the balloon must be paid at that time. The balloon will be the remainder of the amortization of 27% leaving $127,000 ($47,250 amortized). In order to achieve financing leverage, we should estimate our position with refinancing the first mortgage in ten years instead of fifteen years. The first mortgage will amortize 30.5% at the end of ten years, or $77,000. Our situation at the ten year mark will be as follows:

1st mtge. remainder	$143,000
2nd mtge. remainder	127,000
	$270,000

In order to pay off the second mortgage and refinance the first mortgage, we will require a new first mortgage of $270,000. A mortgage of $220,000 would be a maximum for this type of property. The owner then must secure a second mortgage in the amount of $50,000. The rate of interest plus a discount will of course be increased, but with the second decreased by $125,000 the profit will actually be greater.

Weak Areas Are Poor Risks

Income averages $275 F.F. which would place this property in the "Good Neighborhood" category. All of the tenants have posted two months' security with the landlord. In theory, this money is left in trust for the faithful performance of the lease. Two months' rent comes to $840 per tenant. Rerenting a store in the event of a broken lease on only a five year basis would come to $900 brokerage. Undoubtedly there would also be the additional expense of a vacancy for at least 30 days. We now see that two months' security covers some of the reletting expense, but not all. I might add that while this property has two months' security from the tenants, the norm is three months. The supermarket has posted no security because the landlord was not concerned with an AAA-1 tenancy not honoring its lease. We note that the tenants have options at higher rentals, but these increases will be offset by tax increases. In fact the lack of a tax stop is the only real weakness that the property presents. However, the options do give some help. Even if a tenant vacates or does not exercise his option, the rentals would, in this type of property, probably escalate enough to offset the probability of real estate tax increases, reducing the cash flow.

Are The Expenses True?

Expenses in a taxpayer contain only one item that cannot be determined by bill. This item is repairs and maintenance. Your repairs consist of structural, roof and parking field repairs. For the roof, I would recommend putting away $350 per year toward a new roof. I would put away an additional $350 a year to be used to repair pot holes in the parking field. Another $200 per year is put away for structural repairs. This property is located in El Centro, California, so we do not have the problem of snow removal. If this property were located in a northern area such as upstate New York, it would be necessary to include snow removal in the expenses. The amount charged to snow removal is a variable and depends upon area. A reasonable figure would be $400-500 per annum. I want to stress that the expenses outlined are the bare minimum that an owner can expect to spend. The parking lot should be cleaned at least every other month, and the cost should be about $500 per annum. Calculating our repairs and maintenance figure we find that the figure is low by about $500. We will adjust this later.

First mortgage expenses are outlined in the mortgage agreement and consequently leave no room for change.

Real estate taxes can easily be checked by inquiring at the municipal Board of Assessor's Office for the assessment and the rate. By multiplying, you will arrive at the tax. You can look at the owner's last tax bill, but the danger exists that either the assessment or the rate may have subsequently been increased.

Water is in the same category as taxes in that the last water bill may not reflect subsequent increases. Any city water department will be happy to cooperate with you.

Watch For Blanket Policies

Insurance should be checked by having your own insurance man check the latest rates. Also, make sure that the figure given is for fire and liability. In some instances, you will run up against a large property owner who has a blanket policy. The man may own, say, ten taxpayers and pay a premium of $7,000 per annum. When offering a single building for sale he will, assuming all of reasonably equal size, apportion his premium at $700. The arithmetic is correct, but only for the holder of a blanket policy who receives a lower rate. It will be necessary to have your own broker get you a rate for the individual building.

Price of the property is $470,000 with $75,000 cash and the balance in terms. Let us analyze what we have.

Total price		$470,000
1st Mortgage	$220,000	
Cash required	75,000	$295,000
Balance for P.M. 2nd Mtge.		$175,000

Our P.M. 2nd mortgage is in the amount of $175,000. The usual terms for a P.M. mortgage are 6% interest and 2% amortization. This is an arbitrary figure, which may be more or less. The 6 and 2 figure has stood up for a considerable number of years. The P.M. mortgage is after all an accommodation that is tailored to make a deal. If the mortgage interest rate were to fall to 6% or less, then the P.M. rate of interest would of course follow the decline. We now have a $175,000 P.M. mortgage at 6% interest and 2% amortization that must be deducted from the present net, as follows:

Net return	$23,500
Int. & amtz, P.M. 2nd Mtge.	14,000
Cash Flow	$ 9,500

Our bottom line is $9,500 with a cash equity of $75,000. Our percentage of return on equity is figured on a yield of $9,000 because we added an additional $500 to the expenses. The return on equity is 12%. Based upon a 6% prime rate, this would appear to be an excellent return. Ordinarily a taxpayer would be expected to bring in 13%, but because of the safety factor involved in having $30,000 rent from an AAA-1 tenancy, we can readily accept a yield of 12%.

Additional Points

When you search for a good taxpayer investment, you will be tempted—tempted to pick up a bargain. Generally bargains fall into several types of taxpayers. These are the very types that I have recommended you avoid. Do not let a 20% yield warp your good judgment.

As a general rule, I do not like taxpayers without basements. If you must purchase a taxpayer without a basement, make sure that it has a depth of at least 80'. This enables the tenant to partition a portion of the rear for storage. The taxpayer without a basement will often preclude the leasing of a supermarket. The markets require basements of the same size as the retail area. You can't even build additional space or you will be taking away parking and digging a basement becomes quite costly.

I have avoided, up to now, any mention of the two story taxpayer with offices on the second floor. I believe that the two story taxpayer destroys the modern concept of taxpayer ownership. Today's buyer insists, and rightfully so, on owning a self-operating building. A taxpayer with offices on the second floor defeats this purpose in that heat must be supplied to the office tenants and there is cleaning of stairwells, corridors, lavatories and sometimes the offices themselves. Another point to consider is that in the finest of retail areas boasting 100% store occupancy, you will find a substantial amount of second floor space available. I know of a 50' x 75' taxpayer on a truly fine retail block that commands $1,500 F.F. and has a second story leased to a beauty school at $3.00 sq. ft. In order to lease the second floor, the building department required the stairway to be 6' wide. At $1,500 F.F., this was a loss of $9,000 per annum. The second floor rental came to $11,250, but with the additional services required and the additional insurance and real estate taxes, the second floor actually lost money for the landlord. In addition, the landlord did not have the coveted self-operating building.

What To Look For

1. Look for omitted items.
2. Avoid retail neighborhoods changing to industrial.
3. Avoid weak and poor-rated neighborhoods.
4. Avoid buildings that supply heat and/or services to tenants.
5. Do not purchase buildings with wet basements.
6. Check your expenses.
7. You can bend a little on the return if the building has a good safety factor.

Carefully scrutinize offerings for tell-tale signs of property weakness or deterioration. These signs are easily distinguishable. Some of them are as follows:

Numerous month to month tenancies
Several vacancies
Mortgages due within 90 days or less
Tenants paying less than lease agreement
Non-retail tenancies; plumbers, storage, manufacturing, etc.
Parking problems

These weakness problems do not make it mandatory that a property be rejected, but there should be a reflection in the price.

Look for taxpayers that have a proper cash requirement. A proper cash requirement is a maximum of two times the gross rental. It must be remembered that one prime object is to purchase as large a taxpayer as possible with the least amount of money. The perfect situation is to invest 10% of the purchase price in cash. When this is not possible the cash should be held down to a maximum of two times the gross rental.

15

How To Get In On The Shopping Center Phenomenon

The extraordinary development of the shopping center since the termination of World War II has been a modern day miracle. From a few strip centers in the early forties there has been a development to approximately 11,500 large centers today. In addition, the best available figures estimate a growth in shopping centers within the next five years to 20,000 centers. Among the centers to be built will be a great many regional centers, each having between two to four department stores plus 75 to 100 smaller stores.

The tremendous influx of regional and large suburban centers will constitute a large number of ultra modern shopping complexes that before this time were not available to many smaller localities.

In addition to the tremendous influx of new centers there is an unusually large amount of modernization, enlarging and general overhauling of older centers. One of the major improvements is the addition of enclosed malls wherever possible. All of this construction has served and will continue to serve one of the nation's most extensive industries—shopping centers.

Department Stores Are The Key

The key to the majority of large shopping centers is the department store or stores. Today most regionals boast between two to four department stores. The department stores' investment is greater than the builders' and is exceeded only by the financial institutions' investment. The balance of the 75 to 100 stores in a regional does not invest as much as a single department store of say 200,000 feet.

The amount of a department store's investment is a little known item. Even experienced shopping center builders are not fully aware of the colossal investment made. Depending upon the type of department store (discount, general, junior, etc.) the opening price per square foot varies from $40.00 to $60.00 per square foot. This figure includes fixtures, stock, opening expenses, financing credit accounts, bank financing, payrolls, etc. A 200,000 square foot unit would cost approximately $8,000,000 to $12,000,000. These figures are startling but true.

Centers Come In Different Types

I have frequently been asked for the definition of a shopping center. Years ago this would have been a rather simple task—a group of stores, under a single management, with on-premises parking. Today, the definition is greatly complicated. Shopping centers are divided into three separate groups: regional, suburban and strip centers.

The strip center is the pre-World War II throwback. Basically, this is a line of stores, generally four to five to as many as ten or eleven. The anchor store is usually a chain supermarket, and the others are generally service stores. Most of the strip centers are built on about one acre of land.

The suburban center is larger than the strip and will contain between 200,000 to 400,000 square feet of building. The plot varies between twenty acres and thirty-five acres. The anchor generally is a 100,000 foot department or junior department store, with a great many of the suburban centers being Searstown Shopping Centers. Others have J.C. Penney or W.T. Grant as their anchor store. The suburban centers may have as few as fifteen stores and as many as twenty-five.

The regional center is the biggest and the best. Many of the chains feel that occupancy in a large regional is the panacea for instant success. The true regionals contain between 800,000 feet to 1,200,000 feet of building and are situated upon 100 to 150 acres of land. Today's regionals boast from two to four major department stores plus sixty to one hundred other stores of all types. The remarkable part of it all is that the large regionals do seem, based upon their records, to spell instant success.

Check Tenants' Leases

When purchasing a shopping center it is important to make a complete check of the tenant leases. The content of the leases may be of great importance in creating future cash flow, or in retarding same. The more important lease provisions are as follows:

(a) **Increased costs:** To prevent a diminishing profit structure it is essential that leases contain provisions providing stop gaps for taxes, repairs, maintenance and insurance. It is entirely possible that this may be your most important lease clause. I personally know of a Long Island Shopping Center that has had practically 100% occupancy for over 15 years, but the property is presently in the hands of the lending institution. The major leases were of long term duration with minimal increases. There were no stops for taxes, repairs, maintenance or insurance. The expenses outran the income. Even the rental increases were not enough to prevent a deficit cash flow. This situation is especially prevalent among older shopping centers. Some years ago it was not fashionable for a landlord to protect his investment through expense stop gaps. It was expected that nominal rental increases would be sufficient to maintain a status quo in regard to cash flow. This proved not to be true. This situation prevails all over the United States. I

have had on occasion the opportunity to discuss this
particular problem at seminars, conventions and,
during the general course of business, with brokers and
investors. All agreed that the problem was not unique
to any particular sector and should be avoided.

(b) **Omit straight percentage leases:** A straight percentage lease has many drawbacks. A major drawback
is the saleability of the property. Prospective purchasers are prone to give only partial credit for
percentage income. Lending institutions frown upon
straight percentage leases. The criterion which loan
committees use to evaluate percentages is to give
minimum weight to these leases. If a major tenant is
on a percentage only, then the prospective buyer should
be very careful for the reason that in many instances the
landlord has completely surrendered in order to
achieve a particular tenancy. This is a definite sign of
negotiating weakness.

(c) **There should be few "exclusive clauses":** During
the early years, the growing years of the shopping
center, the centers were small. The majority of the
centers had a supermarket plus five to six service
stores. At that time it was possible to give exclusives.
However, during the passing years two notable
changes took place. The centers increased in size and
the number of stores grew to as many as 150 in large
regional centers. At the same time the retail tenancy
began to expand their lines and today they overlap
considerably. Giving exclusives is not only impractical
but faulty business. It has been proven that the public
prefers to shop where it has a wide choice. If a
shopper is, for example, looking to buy a pair of
shoes he will prefer shopping where he has access to a
number of shoe stores rather than a single shoe store.
Exclusives must be avoided because among other
problems they create law suits.

(d) **Franchise tenants—get guarantee.** Since the 1960's
many fine franchise firms have come into being.
These are well run, capable, and financially stable
companies. Occasionally there are weak links—the
franchisee. (In order to insure faithful performance of

a lease it is necessary to get a lease guarantee from the parent company.) Of equal importance is the attitude of the lending institutions, who feel they have greater safety with well guaranteed leases and consequently make more advantageous loans.

(e) **Percentage clauses a must—with variants.** Theoretically various expense stop gaps take care of increased expenses and maintain a non-changeable cash flow. All things being equal this last statement appears quite basic. The statement is both true and false at the same time. It is quite true that maintaining stops on various expenses can maintain cash flow. However, inflation can erode the dollar value of the cash flow. It is because of the constant inflationary climate that we are in that an equalizer is necessary in order to prevent possible erosion of this income. The percentage lease serves this purpose. The percentage clause is sometimes objectionable to the tenant. The objection can on occasion be tempered or the objections completely removed through the use of a variant. For example, any overage earned by the landlord through a percentage lease clause may be reduced in the amount of other monies paid for tax increases, etc. This may not be the perfect situation, but it is a reasonably negotiated situation.

(f) **Length of leases may be vital.** How long should a lease be? This is a question of tremendous importance in that it tends to retain the original chain mix and allows for satellite changes within a reasonable time. I prefer long leases for the major tenants—this holds the main attractions together. It is the mix of major tenancies that creates active shopping centers. The satellite tenancy is always an intangible. The satellites are important for several reasons. First, they pay a far greater per square foot rental than the majors. Secondly, they complement the majors and aid the drawing power. The satellites are, in many instances, more difficult to work into the proper mix and consequently changes are sometimes called for. In order to keep the satellite tenancy flexible five year leases are suggested. The lending institutions are concerned primarily with strong chains and if the property has a mix with 65% chain tenancy the bankers will look favorably upon a mortgage application.

(g) **Radius clauses—not fatal.** I have seen landlords fight heroically against the radius clause. I have seen tenants fight desperately for the radius clause. Personally I believe that the radius clause has long been outmoded and of minimal value. I cannot recall many builders constructing one shopping center on top of another. On the other hand it is a proven fact that a concentration of shopping has an added drain.

(h) **Continuous business operation a must.** Shopping centers both large and small all have one or more main draws. When an anchor draw closes down in a big shopping center it may hurt the center badly. However, when the major draw of a small shopping center closes down it invariably destroys the retail draw and subsequently the center. About the only leeway that may be permitted is allowing the tenant to substitute another tenant in the same business and with like financial stability.

(i) **Merchants' Association is a necessary evil.** It always behooves a landlord to ask a tenant to spend additional monies. The majority of the tenancy invariably are in favor of the Merchant's Association. The anchor tenants sometimes feel that they are better off doing their own advertising. On the other hand some of the individual tenants who profit greatly from the Merchants' Association are going along reluctantly. Their feeling is that they are spending money unnecessarily. The Merchants' Association is vital and must be maintained. The only guarantee of performance is for each lease to contain an adequate clause guaranteeing it.

(j) **Should department stores control tenant mix?** This is a most difficult problem. First, the department store people are true professionals who are aware of what is proper for a shopping center. On the other hand the landlord may have vacancies that are impossible to fill if tenancy is restricted by a mix formula. The problem can, on occasion, become quite knotty when the landlord feels that the department store is unreasonable and the department store feels that the landlord is undercutting the tenancy in filling vacant units. The best solution, I have found, is to have each side appoint an arbitrator to pass judgment on any new tenancy. In the event that the two arbitrators cannot agree, a third is selected by the original two.

I do not want to create the impression that all ten items specified as of much significance to leases must be 100% in favor of the landlord. This would be unusual as there are few faultless deals. When you are able to achieve 70% of these items then the leases are in order. I also strongly suggest the services of an experienced real estate attorney.

Insurance Guarantees Increase Value

No communication about shopping centers can possibly be complete without mentioning the extent that insurance rent guarantees do for shopping center owners.

1. Insurance guarantee creates AAA-1 tenancy for landlord, even if tenant is an individual.
2. Guaranteed tenancy creates an opportunity for an owner to achieve most advantageous terms with lenders.
3. The guarantee increases the economic value of the shopping center in that the center may be sold to show a maximum yield. Where prior economic value is guaranteed, property may achieve as much as a 4% greater yield. This condition may mean a 50% increase in cash over financing.
4. Insurance guarantee creates carefree ownership.
5. Because of an insurance guarantee a tenant may pay a lower rental and thus have a more secure business.

How To Beat The System

Many choice shopping center sites are quite expensive. These sites are usually located on a perimeter just outside of town and cater to the automobile trade. There are wiley old foxes who love to beat the system. Why pay top dollar for land if there may be a way to build the same shopping center on cheaper land? I know of one smart shopping center builder who did find a way to beat the system. I will explain how this man, Gus D., beat the system. Follow the illustration provided and it will be easy to understand the thinking of Gus D. Shopping centers are generally built outside of town, on the main highways, not because the exterior locations are better, but because the main street locations are too expensive to build and often provide inadequate parking.

My illustration is actually the layout of a medium size mid-western town. This layout is not an organized result of systematic town planning. Many towns start developing around main street store property and develop in a similar manner. The banks and office buildings are extensions of the main street. I have provided the other streets names merely for identification purposes.

As with many main streets, they became so because the main roads and highways converge at this point. The closest adjacent streets usually have little or no retail strength. These areas usually contain run down stores. You know the type—churches, machine shops, used office furniture, etc. The main street rentals are $6-$7.00 per front foot and both South First Street and North First Street rentals run $100 to $125 per front foot. Knowing all this Gus proceeded by comparing land prices. Main street land was not available. The area was completely built up. The only way to purchase land was to purchase existing buildings at top prices. Even this method could contain additional problems; some tenants had long term leases. If possible, these leases would have to be purchased for large sums of money.

Gus D. reasoned that South First Street was just as good a location as Main Street if developed properly. While the main highways ran into Main Street, Gus realized that both Avenue A and Avenue B were vitally important to his plan, because these were wide, well traveled streets that ran directly into the residential area—where the customers lived. Gus assembled two square blocks: South First Street to South Third Street and Avenue A to Avenue B. Each block runs 500' x 250', the two blocks having a total area of 250,000 square feet. Gus developed a nice two story shopping center which proved to be quite successful. Not only was the shopping center successful, but the stores along South First Street doubled in value.

Gus' purchase price averaged $2.00 per square foot plus another $.50 per square foot for demolition. The suburban shopping center properties in the area were selling for $200,000 per acre or approxi-

ILLUSTRATION

NORTH 1st STREET

| Post Office | Secondary stores

100% stores | Banks, etc. |

MAIN STREET

| Office
Buildings | 100% Stores

Secondary stores | Office
Buildings |

Avenue A   **SOUTH 1st STREET**   Avenue B

| Town
Parking | Secondary stores

Old Loft Buildings | Town
Parking |

SOUTH 2nd STREET

| | Run-Down Tenements | |

SOUTH 3rd STREET

mately $4.50 per square foot. The cash saving on six acres came to approximately $575,000. The difference in the land cost permitted Gus to mortgage out. (I have nothing but admiration for a man like Gus D. who had a dream, saw an opportunity and seized the proposition. The opportunity was available to anyone else who wished to take it.)

Buy tomorrow's real estate today. Success in the shopping center field seems to be, to a great degree, attached to the aforementioned statement. Those who purchase tomorrow's future today seem to have it made. How is this done? To begin with, a careful study of shopping centers discloses the fact that as people move so do shopping centers. Actually, the shopping centers follow the people.

Using New York City as an example the typical growth pattern follows. Manhattan was the first borough to become saturated with people. Fifth Avenue became the mecca to serve these people. The bulging population forced people to move again, to Brooklyn. Once more a new shopping area was created to serve the increasing population—Fulton Street. Again the story repeated itself and overpopulation caused people to move anew, this time to Nassau County. The center was the Green Acres Regional Shopping Center. Our growing population continued and again people moved, this time to the areas surrounding Garden City. The Roosevelt Field Regional Shopping Center came into being. The situation continues to repeat itself and new centers continue to spring up. This pattern is being repeated in thousands of areas throughout the country and thousands of new centers are being created. I might add that the overwhelming majority of these centers have been successful.

Observing your surroundings could be a great aid in creating a successful shopping center. I know of one man who was eminently successful in this role. After having been a bricklayer for many years he decided to go into business for himself, and built a number of successful taxpayers. Money was only a means to an end, because his real dream was to create big, successful shopping centers. This man, Big Gus, eventually achieved his dream.

The secret of Big Gus' success was relatively simple. Gus would take a main highway out of town, driving until he reached one of those local farm stands. If the stand was located on a corner and was doing a brisk business in the sale of vegetables, Gus felt that the parcel was suitable for a shopping center. Gus would then proceed to purchase the farm. If the acreage was too big for a center, all the better; Gus would sell the excess acreage for one family homes and use the remainder for a shopping center. The formula was simple, but fantastically successful. I personally have always had more confidence in Gus' system than in many high priced feasibility studies. A successful formula is most difficult to beat. I have also found that most times it is advantageous to be an imitator rather than an innovator.

16

Multiplying Your Assets Through Marginal Properties

Buy marginal properties. Does this statement sound like financial disaster? Don't believe it. We rarely think about it, but any item that consumers, investors or what-have-you purchase will be subject to people's whims. Practically speaking these whims come from boredom and a desire for change. This desire for change may come about in three ways.

        A—Actual need for change.
        B—Product makers creating the desire for change.
        C—Public opinion.

Real estate-wise, the most effective method for changing of styles and trends is public opinion. To a large degree the public's opinion is pliable, and as a consequence, easily molded by news media. The image has been built slowly and craftily into a presumed gospel. Many people believe that older, worn out areas mean financial chaos and further decay. This is a dangerous lie because it tells a half truth. Admittedly older neighborhoods are financially risky ventures. Admittedly, landlords and tenants have problems with each other and will, in all probability, continue to have uncertainties. So what? This is only a partial view of this picture.

"Blighted Areas"–Beautiful Real Estate

The other side of the coin is the so called "blighted" areas. Despite their age and older buildings, these regions generally are valuable, densely populated areas. These areas are occupied by blue collar workers, people making more money than many of the white collar workers. The 75% to 100% "blighted" areas are good investments. These properties continue to be outstanding buys as long as the news media accentuate the lower end and neglect the middle and upper end of these areas like Jamaica, Queens. Jamaica Avenue has managed to hold its own against the newer shopping centers. Strangely, it has not developed into a battle between an older street and a new shopping center. Both the new centers and the older street have been successful. The area adjacent to Jamaica Avenue was composed of ancient one and two family homes. Enterprising builders came into the area and erected brand new elevator apartment buildings. The buildings were successful. The secret is that the key to so-called marginal areas is transportation. The area caters to a group who tends to congregate around good transportation. These are people who either do not have automobiles or only use their cars on Sunday. Consequently transportation is of prime importance.

Jamaica Avenue has been a prime shopping street for a great many years and continued through the great building upheaval and construction tumult of the sixties. It carried into the seventies and has continued to thrive. During the 1950's stores along this street were renting for $800 to $900 per front foot per annum. The 1970's now show that the same retail units are commanding rentals of $1,500 per front foot per annum. The increased commercial rentals plus the luxury apartment buildings must prove, to even the worst skeptic, that the older neighborhoods contain some good real estate. Regardless of how the balance of the area fares the focal points of good transportation will continue to appreciate. The tragedy is that many investors did and still do believe the big lie. These half truths have convinced many investors, now holding older real estate that now is the time to get out.

Do not sell if you are an owner of good property in an old neighborhood, because you will be giving away good real estate. Furthermore, there is a poor sellers market because prospective purchasers are wary. These two situations enable an astute purchaser to buy old "blighted" real estate at bargain prices.

Can You Sell Marginal Real Estate?

A business associate of mine was offered a commercial property near a fantastic older shopping street. The building had been vacant for some time and had been vandalized quite badly. The building was actually an eyesore. The last tenant was a factory. It had front parking for truck loading because the plot was an interior parcel and there was no road to the rear. The last tenancy had been some ten years prior. The property was owned by a large estate and it seemed that there was little interest in it.

The property itself was not in the 100% block, but close to the 100% area. In fact the building was eight blocks from the center of the action. The area was old and getting shabby, but it did have an automobile traffic count of 35,000 cars per 24 hour day, and it was on a subway block. The owners of the property felt that the only value the property had was land value, and very little at that. There was no "for sale" sign on the property.

My friend was aware of the value of good marginal property and wanted to own this real estate. I was asked to help with the purchase of the property. I spoke with the attorney representing the owners and was told that he was only interested in selling at a price of $50,000—all cash. The sudden value was probably caused by a newspaper article proposing this general area as suitable for urban renewal. I waited some six months until I felt that the owners would realize that the urban renewal mentioned in the newspapers was only a dream. I went back to the attorney and surprisingly was advised that they had decided to maintain the $50,000 price. My friend did not have $50,000. Rather than admit defeat I tried to put together a deal.

I approached a number of drive-in restaurant chains and some responded affirmatively. The other chains rejected the area because it was too far from the 100% area. Many chains had obviously bought the propaganda that the older neighborhoods were played out. Finally I connected—a convenience type market was interested in the location and they offered to pay $20,000 per annum net net for twenty years. The only hitch was that they wanted the building repaired and altered to their specifications. The cost would be $30,000. I began to smell the makings of a deal.

Negotiations began and I offered the landlord $15,000 per annun net net if he would spend the $30,000 to alter and renovate the property. The landlord, over the term of the lease, would be getting a gross of $300,000 and his net profit would be $270,000 plus retaining ownership of the property. I consummated for my friend a long term lease with the landlord and simultaneously signed a lease with the grocery chain. To clarify the picture let me explain that in effect the landlord now has a lease with my friend, who had subleased to the grocery chain. The owner was aware of my negotiations with the grocery chain at all times.

A Good Deal For Everyone

This deal was beautiful for everyone. The landlord would net $270,000 instead of selling the property for $50,000. The grocery chain was delighted with the location, because it was a real money maker. I made a nice brokerage commission. My friend would collect $5,000 per annum for 20 years or a total of $100,000. He had absolutely no investment except my commission. If you want to work at it, good properties may sometimes be controlled with little or no investment.

Marginal Properties Offer Possibilities

The older type neighborhood store tenant has long been in lower end locations a marginal operator. I refer specifically to the so-called 50% locations. These properties can, in many instances, be purchased at real bargain prices. I have seen this type property show a 20% yield over financing. The basic reason for these bargains is that a goodly segment of the investing public has been brainwashed into avoiding older properties. Another reason for the high equity yield is that some of the tenants have problems paying their rent. This may be turned into an asset.

I know a Florida real estate operator who only purchases 50% properties in the older type neighborhoods. The secret of his success is an understanding of the reasons why many of these merchants have difficulty. My friend realized that the two prime reasons for tenant problems are:

A—Underfinancing
B—Inexperience

This real estate operator uses the facilities of the government to improve his property. The underfinancing situation is referred to the Small Business Administration, which has been very helpful in aiding under-financed small business firms. As for the problem of inexperience —this is also taken care of by the government. The Federal government has lists of thousands of retired, successful businessmen who volunteer their services. By utilization of these two agencies the operator has made a fortune. The strange part of it all is that these two agencies are widely known and readily available yet rarely turned to advantage by realty investors.

Not only can money be made with the commercial properties, in these districts, but also with the residential properties—apartment buildings. The apartment buildings in these neighborhoods are composed of two types: very old and very new. The new buildings are successful because they are new and they meet the criterion of being near good transportation. But the old buildings are where the sleepers are. The uninformed pseudo-experts would have you believe that rehabilitating older buildings is quite costly. The exorbitant cost is created because all the apartments must be remodeled and the large apartments cut up into smaller ones. This is pure nonsense and absolutely untrue. Years ago there was a large demand for smaller units, but today the situation is reversed. The six and seven room apartments are now in big demand. Luckily these older buildings contain many large units. Areas to be renovated include the kitchen, bathroom and main lobby. The rest of the building becomes quite attractive because of its unique period. Even after the expense of alterations, relocation of tenants, new financing, etc., the return on equity will be in the neighborhood of 15%-18%. This is as good a return as is possible to achieve.

Some of the renovation specialists I know have a system that is unbeatable—resulting in a money making building each time. A great many of the cities with older residential areas are quite proud of their historical backgrounds. Almost all of the larger cities have historical societies. These societies name many buildings in the older areas to be preserved as historical landmarks. Mostly these properties are architectural mementos of the past. Despite their being in old, and often run-down neighborhoods, tenants love these buildings because of their snob appeal. Consequently these old timers are ideal for purchase and renovation. The older the buildings, the more the tenants love them. Some of these buildings are of great historical interest. As an example there is one block in Brooklyn that has an entire blockfront of old carriage houses. The interiors have all been renovated and the ones that I have been inside of are really fantastic. The exteriors are untouched and remain as they were one hundred years ago. The last quotation I heard for one of these houses was $70,000. Who can say what a one-of-a-kind item is worth? The tenants take pride in their individual buildings and thus the neighborhood may be improved. Older neighborhoods seem to possess endless means for rehabilitation. An interesting method is the cooperative. The apartments are sold, in a large majority, to the existing tenancy. The prime criterion that is of importance to the entrepreneur is that the building best suited for conversion to a co-op must be an older but formerly elegant property. Over the years it has been found that the run-of-the-mill buildings are not suitable because they are not readily saleable. Again, however, the building must be in close proximity to transportation.

Another source of investment to be considered in older neighborhoods is the attached one family dwellings. These buildings are either brick or brownstone, three to four stories high and containing 12-14 rooms. This type building is in great demand as town houses. The purchasers delight in removing the many coats of paint from the wood trim in order to expose beautiful mahogany or oak. Tenants also revel in the admirable wood carved fireplaces and lofty ceilings. The older the building the easier the apartments are to sell.

In the older neighborhoods we also find large cottages, on 40′ — 100′ x 100′ plots. These properties are of no interest for one family home prospects. The buildings are too large and require too much work to maintain. Also, other than town houses, the one family buyer is interested in new or reasonably new structures in suburban areas—definitely not old run-down urban areas. There is a new use for these buildings. Investors purchase these buildings, make alterations to conform with fire department and building department regulations and then lease them to rooming house operators. Transportation accessibility is not as important to this type operator as it is to the others previously mentioned.

One investor, Frank R., had a very nice little operation that he practically had a patent on. Frank would choose a choice traffic congregation point, usually one hundred feet from the business property, but close enough to the transportation hub to be effective. Purchasing one hundred feet from the business property meant that instead of purchasing expensive commercial property he could buy inexpensive residential property. Frank would get options on five to six adjacent one family residences with a minimum of two hundred feet frontage, apply for rezoning to a parking lot use, and if successful erect a parking lot on the premises. Frank would then sell the property to a parking operator.

Investors have had absolutely extraordinary success with investments in these so-called old, "blighted" areas. Within these areas great fortunes may be made. Great fortune is there for the picking.

What To Look For

Marginal properties, to a great degree, must be handled differently from other types. Marginal properties have different characteristics. One of these characteristics is the question of financing. Financing is not often available from lending institutions. This lack of institutional financing can be a big plus, an advantage that may not be available in the so called better type properties. The so called better type properties will normally have conventional institutional financing—financing that is locked in as to amount of loan and amount of interest rate.

Now what about the marginal properties? Well, these properties have the advantage of not being able to get conventional financing. Because of this "problem" sellers find it necessary to take back purchase money mortgages. Because of their very nature, purchase money mortgages are negotiable. Historically, purchase money mortgages are written at lower interest and amortization rates. This situation will seem to enhance profits.

In order to fully take advantage of the purchase money mortgage the buyer should look for free and clear properties, and there are many in this category.

17

How To Create Big Profits—
Without Increasing Rentals

I suppose, as we all know, the eternal search by investors is to secure a "bargain." A bargain, strictly defined, is the purchase of a property for less than market value. Such a property, it follows, could then be sold at market price for a profit. So let us scurry about for bargains and make a fortune. Of course I am jesting. Bargains, like hidden treasures, are difficult to come by. Consequently, we are forced to devise other methods that lead to profits and build the foundations for fortunes. During the ordinary course of events we are able to purchase properties at fair market value and if we can improve upon the purchase we are afforded the opportunity of selling at a profit. The improvement of property is commonly thought to be the increasing of the gross rental and thereby increasing the cash flow. With a greater cash flow the property may demand a greater price. I have found that there are other methods of increasing the market value of investment properties without increasing the gross rentals.

It may be difficult to believe, but it is a fact that it is entirely possible to buy investment property and sell at an increase in price without ever increasing rentals. For over twenty five years as a real estate broker, consultant and principal I have watched many people do this very thing. Because of the investment opportunities available today, I firmly hold that the great American frontier lies in the cultivation of real estate investments. Investors may achieve greater success by emulating some of the very interesting patterns herein related of successful investments.

"The purchase of real estate for long term investment." This particular sentence has a nice ring to it. It almost seems to have a sort of religious aura about it. A definition of this sentence is generally understood to mean that through hard work and saving money eventually you will be able to purchase a conservative investment property that will support you in your declining years. For about 95% of the army of investors this is pure nonsense. Security may best be achieved by operating, buying and selling investments. I make this statement fully aware that I am going to disturb a portion of the investment army. The group to be upset will be comprised of some very wealthy and some very aged investors; both groups together comprise about 5% of the total investing population.

The very wealthy and the very aged are minority groups who must be dedicated to their own special problems.

(a) Aged—Have the fear of losing a lifetime of savings. This can cause their adherence to a poor economic policy called "Marrying your property."

(b) Wealthy—Their purchase of properties is dominated by tax situations.

Don't Marry—Sell

I can readily understand the investment plans of the very rich. I can also have sympathy with the investment philosophy of many aged investors. However, under no conditions should the majority (95%) of the other investors be entrapped by a credo that can retard their path toward success. For the great majority, investment must mean the purchase of real estate and holding of the properties only until they can be sold at a reasonable profit. This procedure is to be constantly repeated. The result invariably is an escalation of profits. Do not decide that in your infinite wisdom you have purchased a fantastic property that is to be held for all of your life and then left to your children and grandchildren. In a phrase—don't marry real estate. You cannot go broke taking profits. The tried and true method for creating wealth in real estate is the process of buying and selling—operating.

Improve The Property

The logical question to ask at this point is: How do I purchase investment property and sell at a profit? The answer is to simply improve the property. This may be done either physically or economically. I may be oversimplifying so I will give you an example. I know of a particular case where a man purchased a taxpayer for $100,000, did not increase the gross rental, and still made the property more valuable and consequently sold at a profit. The structure of this property was as follows:

Gross rental		$15,000
Estimated expenses		
Real estate taxes	$3,000	
Water	300	
Insurance	1,200	
Repairs	150	
Int. & amtz.*	3,600	$ 8,250
Cash flow		$ 6,750

* 1st Mortgage: $25,000 balance. (originally $45,000). 6% interest and 2% amortization. Due in 5 years. Bank mortgage.

Price: $75,000 cash over existing 1st mortgage, to show 9% on equity.

This particular property was relatively easy to purchase because it had been "shopped around," and was thought by most investors to be somewhat overpriced. Truthfully, the property actually was overpriced and underpriced—both at the same time. The same property can be viewed in a different light by different investors. I believe that real estate investors sometimes are not very different from lovers. I mean that properties sometimes assume values existing only in the eye of the beholder. In the eyes of most investors there was a determination that this property was overpriced because of the meager 9% return. The property looked entirely different to one gentleman who actually purchased this property because he felt that the property was underpriced. Who was right?

Let us follow the workings of the purchaser and see how he created a profit for himself. This investor, I would like to inject, was not a sophisticated buyer, but an owner of a parking lot with little real estate experience. Actually he had bought and sold two small taxpayers, this transaction being, by far, his biggest deal. To continue, a new first mortgage was arranged for in the identical amount ($25,000) and at the same terms, 6% interest and 2% amortization. This recasting of the financing reduced the mortgage payment by $1,600 per annum and created an 11% yield on equity for the purchaser. The property had a fair market value of 10% and was easily sold for $83,500, the new cash flow being $8,350. Net profit on this transaction, to the investor, was $8,500. The constant improvement of your property, shown in this example through financing, will aid in the creation of greater wealth.

Physical Improvement Aids Profits

An obvious aid to profit that I previously mentioned entails physical improvement of the property. Pursuing this vein, I know of an investor who purchased a well-built warehouse with a AAA-1 tenancy. The building may be best described as a one story, garage type property. Structurally the building was sound. The appearance of the building created exactly the opposite impression. The overhead garage door, situated at the front of the building, had several panes of wood knocked out. The remainder of the front of the building had never been painted and the overall picture was a sad one. The windows were in good shape, but they too had missing panes of glass. To many prospective purchasers, who examined the building, the comments ranged from "cost a fortune to fix up," to "structurally unsound." In spite of its appearance the building eventually was sold. The new owner had the broken window panes replaced, installed plywood squares where they were missing from the garage door, and had the front of the building painted. The entire cost for the "renovation" was less than $100. The building was purchased at a price of $50,000 and showed a return on equity of 10% free and clear. The property was resold after the "renovation" for $55,000, the new return being 9.1%. The cash profit to the seller was $5,000. Not bad, when you consider that less than $100 was spent to spruce up the building. Through the use of small, cosmetic improvements the value of this property had been increased without any increase in rental or cash flow.

An interesting sidelight to this transaction was that the building had originally been owned by the tenant, the tenant being a large paint and hardware concern. The tenant had the supplies and manpower to aid in the improvement of the visual effect this building offered. Failure on their part to spend about $50 (tenant buys supplies at wholesale) cost them $5,000 in price that could have gone into their own pocket if the building had been made properly attractive for a purchaser.

An important consideration in the purchase of any investment property must be the possibility of increasing value without increasing rentals. Please understand, I have nothing against using the procedure of increasing rentals in order to boost property values. However, a great many properties are locked in with no hope of increase. The tenants may have long leases and nothing can be done to increase rents. Then again there is always the possibility that the existing rentals have reached a saturation point, they may be at their maximum. In this type of situation you could rightfully feel stymied. It is a well known fact that the law of diminishing returns usually prevails in preventing landlords from achieving rentals in excess of prevailing market value. Therefore, the method of "improvement" of property can become an important tool in the creation of profit.

By The Grace Of God

Another method of property improvement, without rental increase, is one I like to call "by the grace of God method." Fortunes in real estate are not always made by astute thinkers or brilliant planners. Fortunes are often made by being in the wrong place at the right time. I recall a Korean War veteran who was interested in purchasing a home for his wife and infant child. The plan was to purchase a small frame dwelling on Long Island. After extensive searching in many nearby to New York City Long Island towns, the family came to the realization that they did not have enough money for a "close-in" house. The only alternative seemed to be to look further out on Long Island. Here, too, the down payments required seemed too large for this young family. There was, however, one house being offered for sale at $18,000 and it only required a $1,500 down payment, the balance of the purchase price to be financed on a long term mortgage. The house was quite old, but could be fixed up. The plot was oversized, being three acres. The big drawback was that the house was located on a business street. Not much of a business street, but it did have a lot of automobile traffic and many prospective home buyers avoided it for this very reason. Now, let us shift the scene to five years later. The sleepy little town had seen over 4,000 additional homes built nearby and in the town itself. This business property, consequently, became extremely valuable. The sum and substance of ths story is that the veteran, now five years older, sold the property to a shopping center builder for $200,000. I lost track of the family after they sold out. I have, somehow always wondered if they bought a conventional home, now that they had the down payment, or if they moved further out and bought another residence in a business sector. The possibility of lightning striking twice always exists in the real estate world.

This veteran was a lucky young man. He bought a house and made a fortune. While he was unaware of what he was doing he was buying a property that would improve by itself. He was following a tried and true formula. Buy in the path of progress and the property will improve without your doing a thing. When the ever moving arm of progress reaches your property the value increases. In order to appreciate a gain of this type it is necessary to determine the direction of the population shift and to purchase in the path of these shifts.

Watch For Good Land-To-Building Assessments

An interesting method of increasing value without rental increases is a system used by a high school teacher client of mine. This teacher made more money from dabbling in real estate than he did teaching school. As an investor he had only one formula and stayed with his winning system. Knowing well that either expertise or opportunity was necessary to increase value, he studiously avoided this route. Our man's plan was to purchase properties and sell them at a profit without achieving rental increases. He carefully sought properties that were assessed with the bulk of the assessment being assigned to the building portion. He particularly liked a land-to-building ratio of 1:15. An illustration of the actual mechanics is as follows:

Rental	$24,000
Expenses before mortgage	$16,000
Free and clear net	$ 8,000
1st Mortgage: $30,000 at 7% interest and	
2% amortization	$ 2,700
Cash flow after financing	$ 5,300

Price: $50,000 over 1st mortgage to show 10.6% net on equity.

Note: The property was assessed for $80,000 with $75,000 going toward the building and the remainder toward the land.

Tax picture:	Cash flow after financing	$ 5,300
	Amortization profit	600
	Taxable before depreciation	$ 5,900

The subject building yields $5,900 including amortization. Anyone buying this property who is in a 50% bracket would be able to have good tax shelter. With the 1:15 ratio the amount of building tax free is 93%. The total price is $80,000. Taking 93% we have taxable building amount of $74,000. Taking 3% of this figure we then have a tax deduction of $2,232.

Taxable before depreciation	$5,900
Allowable deduction	2,232
Taxable income	$3,668

The actual taxable income is $3,668. The tax saving is $2,232. For someone in a 50% bracket this is actually a saving of $4,464. People with large salaries who are in high tax brackets constantly seek investments with built-in tax shelter. Our school teacher made a career of seeking this type and in turn selling them to a specialized group of investors.

The ways to make money without increasing rentals are numerous. This is truly a fantastic system when you realize that a building may be purchased, a small improvement made and you are in line for a quick profit. The improvement in the tax shelter system is only in improving the presentation and showing the tax shelter benefits that the particular property has to offer. A good sheltered property will sell for more than the going price. What it all comes down to is that with a small improvement you place yourself in line for a quick profit. What could be easier?

Still another method that has proven quite successful is the real estate tax method. This method is utilized best in certain sets of circumstances, namely, those buildings that are over-assessed. A client of mine made many deals through the application of this method. Whenever this man received an offering from a broker or principal the first thing that he looked for under the expense items was taxes. The assessment will differ in various communities. This does not present much of a problem, because if a few offerings are studied, the local equalization rate may be determined. The client previously referred to did his buying in New Jersey. The assessment range in communities checked was from 25% to 33% of gross income. To be more explicit the amount of tax, dollarwise, was between 25% to 33% of the total income. A great many of these buildings are over-assessed with tax payments as high as 50% of income. How or why these errors occur is of little importance, only they do occur. Where it can be shown that a building is over-assessed the municipal authorities will review the assessment and reduce the tax accordingly. The reduction in tax payments can be quite substantial. A shopping center purchased in eastern New Jersey proved to be a classic example. An illustration follows:

Gross rental	$70,000
Expenses, less taxes	40,000
Profit before taxes	$30,000
Taxes	24,500
Cash flow	$ 5,500

In this instance the real estate taxes are 35% of the gross income. In this particular sector comparable properties were paying taxes of approximately 25% of gross income. An application for reduction of taxes was filled requesting a 10% reduction in tax payment. After a hearing the reduction was granted. The reduction changed the tax payment to $17,500, which increased the cash flow by $7,000. My client had purchased the property to show 11% on equity, paying $50,000 over financing. The property, after the tax reduction, was resold at the same 11% yield. With the increase in the cash flow going to $12,500 the property was sold for $113,000 cash over financing for a profit of $63,000. This property had been improved by an adjustment in taxes. With profits of this type it should be worth every investor's time to carefully check his real estate tax situations.

Things To Remember

(1) You can create big profits without increasing rentals.

(2) Don't marry your property. Operate for profits.

(3) Improve your property to create profits

    (a) By refinancing

    (b) By physical improvement

    (c) By proper presentation of tax shelter benefits

    (d) By applying for reduction of real estate taxes when warranted

    (e) By buying in the path of progress

(4) Luck sometimes plays an important part in the making of fortunes.

What To Look For

Ordinarily profits are made in real estate by increasing gross rentals and consequently net profits. With the increase of net profits there is an increase in value. The increase in revenue can take anywhere from six months to several years. Why not a quicker method?

Quicker methods are available. Easier methods are also available. The easiest methods are as follows.

Recasting financing. The basis of this method is predicated upon looking for buildings with approximately 50% old mortgages. I refer to mortgages that had been placed, say, 15 years ago and are seven to eight years old. All things being equal, this would be ideal for recasting the financing and increasing value.

Another method for producing quick profits is the over-assessed building. I have found that there are tens of thousands of over-assessed buildings throughout the nation. A study of tax structures and simple comparisons will reveal those properties that may be used to your advantage. This is a simple but effective method.

Possibly the easiest method of preparing a property for an increase in value is to "give it a coat of paint." Look for properties with minor cosmetic flaws. These properties are difficult to sell because many buyers have pride of ownership. Bargains are available and should be acquired.

18

Leverage—The Amazing Profit Booster

Leverage, as most people perceive, is the capacity to obtain an advantage by reason of the use of a lever. In real estate our lever is financing. The prime users of leverage are generally operators. Operators are not fly-by-night investors—contrary to a widely held opinion, Operators buy with the purpose of reselling at a profit. Bargains do not abound today and so the operator is forced to purchase ordinary buys and transform them into bargains. In order to lay the basis for the transformation, the operator should only purchase property on the following basis:

      (A) Free and clear properties
      (B) Properties encumbered by a first lien only

Leverage Foundation Is Secondary Financing

It is most often secondary financing that creates the leverage. Third mortgages are passé today and so the property must be unobstructed for the second or leverage mortgage. Properties with existing second mortgages cannot ordinarily be leveraged adequately. Within the past several years leverage has assumed great consequence in the opinion of real estate appraisers and particularly in the opinion of institutional appraisers. Up until several years ago investment properties were only appraised on a free and clear basis. This method has been dropped by many institutional appraisers as being inaccurate; it was held that two identical buildings, adjacent to each other, may have different values. The difference in value may be caused by different financing techniques. Leverage may enhance one building's value as against its adjacent twin. Leverage has recently assumed a certain respectability in having its recognition transcend from operators to banks and insurance companies.

Don't Pay Off The Mortgage

A great many part-time investors do not feel that they have a secure investment until they have fully paid off their mortgage and own their property free and clear. This notion is not a safe, sound investing principle, but a risky, foolhardy idea. I recall Tony O., an ice man, who owned almost a million dollars' worth of real estate. Daily he could be seen along the streets of his city, perched on the back of his truck grinding up ice for various taverns in town. Tony had saved his money and invested regularly for almost fifty years. During this half century Tony had amassed a fortune in real estate. The bulk of the property was owned free and clear. Tony was a firm believer in paying off mortgages and never refinancing.

One day Tony was found dead of a heart attack. Several weeks after his burial his widow, the sole heir, contacted her family lawyer. The lawyer informed the widow that the estate would have a rather large inheritance tax to pay. This at first appeared a minor problem, but the difficulty gradually increased. Tony, it seemed, had left little cash, preferring to use his money in purchasing additional properties and paying off existing mortgages. The widow had a real problem; she needed substantial cash to satisfy government liens.

Mortgage brokers and lending institutions were contacted concerning financing the properties. After some weeks the lawyer and the widow came to the realization that the mortgage market at this point in time was not only poor but practically non-existent. There are periods when lending institutions, for various reasons, make few mortgage loans. This was one of those times; no financing was available.

In order to satisfy the government liens it was necessary to sell off many properties and thoroughly dissipate the estate. Had Tony understood financing and leverage, he could have had a larger cash flow, purchased more properties and have enough cash to pay the government lien; or he could have sold off part of a larger estate and still have a greater estate than what he left behind after taxes.

Keep The Cash Equity Down

The operation of properties is most advantageous when using leverage. A client, Harvey M., had a father who was most thoughtful. He invested the profits from a meat chain in a large suburban shopping center. Upon the death of Harvey's father he inherited the shopping center subject to a first mortgage. Basically the center set-up was as follows:

Gross rental:	$400,000
Expenses:	$ 75,000
Profit free & clear	$325,000
1st mortgage interest & amortization	200,000
($2,000,000 - 8% interest—	
2% amortization)	
Cash flow	$125,000

Figuring on a 10% basis the market value of this center would be:

1st mortgage:	$2,000,000
Cash Equity:	1,225,000
Market Value	$3,725,000

The $3,725,000 value is an interesting price and applicable under ordinary conditions. There is one basic weakness—the amount of cash equity required is $1,225,000 or over three times the gross rental. It would be difficult to sell under these terms. The investment market in a "cash over" transaction historically has been two times the gross rent as a maximum, the range being between 1½-2 times gross rental.

On the open market this property would be difficult to sell. However, a smart operator sensed a potentially advantageous purchase, and the property was purchased at the asking price. The operator without delay placed the property for disposal. However, having a thorough acquaintance of leverage, the operator presented his building on an entirely different principle. The operator's presentation was as follows:

Gross Rent	$400,000
Expenses	75,000
	$325,000
Existing 1st mortgage interest & amortization	200,000
	$125,000
Operators purchase money 2nd mortgage $800,000 at 7% interest and 1% amortization	$ 64,000
Cash Flow	$ 61,000

Price: $610,000 cash over financing

The operator's modification was the addition of a purchase money second mortgage. Suddenly this is a saleable property because the cash requirement is approximately 1½ times the gross rental. Also, there are more buyers with $600,000 than with $1,250,000. So by coming within the market price and increasing the number of potential buyers the operator greatly enhanced his opportunity for consummating a sale.

The property was resold by the operator within two weeks. How did he make out? Well, let's examine the transaction.

Sales Price	$3,410,000
Purchase Price	3,225,000
Profit	$ 185,000

A profit of $185,000 was realized on paper. Actually the operator paid a bonus of $80,000 for the second mortgage. The net cash profit was $150,000. Not bad for two weeks work. Leverage provided a profit through an ingenious shift.

The Insurance Method

Leverage is not a one way street. There are a number of methods of utilizing leverage. One of the more interesting methods of increasing value through the use of leverage is the insurance method. The strange thing about the insurance method is that it is well advertised, but not used often enough. The only reason that I can think of for its lack of use is a failure to understand it fully.

I was involved in a transaction in which the insurance method proved the catalyst in creating additional value. The property involved was a single tenant, net lease with a supermarket. The tenant was a member of a cooperative, but the cooperative had not guaranteed the lease. The lease was with an individual. The rent schedule was as follows:

> $20,000 for first to fifth years
> $25,000 for sixth to tenth years
> $30,000 for eleventh to fifteenth years
> $35,000 for sixteenth to twentieth years

With an individual on the lease, single tenant net leases sold at a 11-12% yield with adequate financing. This property had an $80,000 first mortgage at 8% interest and 1½% amortization, the constant payment being $7,600 per annum. Of course, being a net lease, the tenant paid all expenses. The profit and loss setup was quite simple.

Rental	$20,000
Expenses:	
Interest & amortization	
1st mortgage	$ 7,600
Cash Flow	$12,400

The owner of the property, Big Gus, was interested in selling in order to divide the property with his divorced wife as per a court order. If the property had been sold "as is" at current market prices it would have brought approximately $112,716 over the existing mortgage, an 11% yield on equity. The total price was $192,716. Both the lease and mortgage were in their first year so that there was, for our purposes, no adjustments necessary. I advised against selling via this method.

I recommended to my client that he use the insurance method.

The insurance plan, in my opinion, is a fresh notion in protecting investments for property owners. Frankly, I had never used the insurance method before. I was, however, knowledgeable of the plan. Further, I was familiar with several owners who had used the plan with great success.

The physical maneuvers necessary to secure the insurance were relatively simple. I applied to an insurance company that wrote lease guarantee insurance. The company then made a determination based upon rent, lease, tenant and location. All items proved to be eligible. The company had a policy of writing insurance with a five year minimum and a maximum of fifteen years. I applied for the fifteen year period.

The premium due the insurance company for the lease guarantee insurance is a single premium, paid in advance, for the entire period of the policy. The premium is arrived at by multiplying the gross rental for the entire period insured by a sliding percentage. The range is from 5.4% for a five year policy to 2.8% for a fifteen year policy.

There are interesting features of the policy that I particularly like. First the policy is non-cancellable. Second, the owner of a property may without company approval assign the policy to a purchaser or to a lending institution. The new assured gains all benefits given to the original policy holder.

With the strength of the policy behind the subject property, I began to apply leverage to the deal. The property, prior to the application of leverage, had a fair market value of $192,716. After leverage I expected to increase the market value substantially.

On account of the rent now being guaranteed as against a problematical rental prior to the lease guarantee, the yield on equity, having an increased safety factor, now assumed a 9% rate, this rate being based on comparable properties sold within a reasonable period of time.

With the rental guaranteed, it now becomes possible to average the rent for the first fifteen years of the lease. The average rent was calculated at $25,000 per annum. The building at the present time was set up differently. The new listing was as follows:

Rental (average)	$25,000
Expenses:	
1st mortgage interest & amortization	7,600
*Cash Flow:	$17,400

Calculating on a 9% return on equity the fair market value would be $193,314 cash over the existing $80,000 first mortgage, or a total price of $273,314. The additional market value gained through leverage was as follows:

New Value	$273,314
Previous Value	192,716
	$ 80,598
Less Insurance Cost*	10,500
Increased Value to Seller	$ 70,098

*Rental, 15 years equal	$375,000
Insurant Rate equal	2.8%
Insurance Premium	$ 10,500

Over a lengthy period of time I have learned the merit of leverage. I must admonish, however, that leverage does not always work in all conditions. Properties with two existing mortgages are difficult to leverage. When lease guarantee insurance is used, the tenant must be a reasonably good risk or this too will be difficult to leverage.

Increased Interest, Increased Profit

There is no limit to the amounts of money that may be made by investing in a ball point pen or pencil. With an investment of pennies, literally millions may be made. The writing instrument may then serve its owner well by aiding in the figuring of possible leveraging of properties offered for sale. An excellent example that comes to mind was a property being offered as follows:

Price	$1,500,000
First mortgage	1,200,000
Cash Equity	$ 300,000
Cash Flow	$ 21,000 (7%)

In analyzing the property it was clear that the return on equity was 7%. The property involved was a garden apartment. A return of 7% for this type property was well below the market. The property had been on the market for over a year without any takers.

I, personally, had no interest in the property, because I felt it to be completely overpriced. I had no interest personally nor would I offer the property to a prospect. I completely ignored an overpriced property.

One day Larry W., a well known operator asked me if I knew of any garden apartments for sale in the Los Angeles area. Reluctantly I mentioned the overpriced property, adding that I though it was overpriced and should be passed over. Larry asked for the particulars, which I passed along to him. Approximately ten days later Larry W. called and inquired if the price was firm. I advised him that the owner had been unyielding in his price for over a year, resisting all offers. Larry responded by requesting that I make arrangements for a contract of purchase to be arranged—at the asking price. Surely a sophisticated operator such as Larry W. had not lost his good business sense! The plain truth is that Larry saw a good buy and wanted the property. Larry obviously saw an excellent opportunity to improve the cash flow through leverage.

The leveraging was done by securing different financing. The existing first mortgage had a 6% interest rate and was self-liquidating in 15 years, the annual interest and amortization payment being $116,847.36. Larry W. went to the lending institution and offered to increase the interest rate to 8% if the lending institution would change the mortgage to a thirty year full payout. The bank agreed. The new mortgage payment now is $105,663.66. What happened?

$116,847.36	Old mortgage payment
105,663.66	New mortgage payment
$ 11,183.70	Reduction in mortgage payment
21,000.00	Previous cash flow
$ 32,183.70	New cash flow

The cash flow increased to $32,183.70. The return on equity now became 10.7% which was market value. Larry W., with a good ballpoint pen, had made himself an excellent purchase.

The same operator, Larry W., made another purchase that was absolutely fantastic—the type of deal that investors dream about. He purchased a small shopping center with no cash investment. The shopping center under discussion was structured as follows:

Price:	$1,000,000
Mortgage:	700,000
Equity:	300,000
Cash flow:	30,000

Larry W. purchased the job on a 10% yield on equity. This was a very average buy. Larry then went about restructuring the deal. The existing mortgage was for ten years, with a balloon, at 6½% interest and 5% amortization; the constant payment being $115,000 per annum. Larry was to work out an interesting situation with the present holder of the mortgage. He agreed to increase the interest rate to 8% interest and 2.5% amortization, self-liquidating in twenty years, with a $300,000 increase in the mortgage. The lending institution was delighted because they were getting a higher interest rate and felt reasonably secure because the mortgage was on a self-liquidating basis. The new mortgage payment was approximately the same as the old mortgage payment. The result was that Larry W. had purchased a cash flow of $30,000 with no cash investment.

Among the immediate results created through leverage are the not readily discernible benefits. We can easily determine that leverage creates wealth. However, it must be added to the credit side of leverage that it helps create the tremendously large structures seen throughout our country. The ideas created through leverage provide an amazing number of jobs in the building industry. The work created through leverage has greatly aided in the distribution of funds through banks, pension funds and insurance companies. Leverage contributes substantially to the real estate and construction industries.

Leverage Must Be Used Properly

I must, however, advise that there are some disadvantages to leveraging. Where an owner has a thin equity he can be in real trouble if there is even a small economic breeze, let alone a real financial storm. Poor management must also be watched for as it may readily eliminate an owner with a thin equity. Leverage also attracts a certain weak element—the shoestring operator who tries to build or purchase beyond his means through leveraging. Leverage, to produce lasting results, must be used discriminately. When properly used, leverage is a very useful tool.

To my mind the most interesting feature concerning leverage is its unique ability to take two identical properties adjacent to each other and make one property more valuable than its twin. Leverage must be considered one of the great financial tools used to accelerate profits.

What To Look For

For many years leverage appeared to be the exclusive domain of operators and other professionals. There is no reason why the general public cannot participate in this money maker.

To participate in the leverage advantages it is necessary to look for properties that lend themselves toward leverage. Finding such properties is not difficult. The entire trick to leverage is financing. Properties that particularly lend themselves to this have the following characteristics.

> Free and clear
> First mortgages only
> Low cash equity
> Insured rentals
> Refinanced

With the various options available it would appear that candidates for leveraged properties are reasonably easy to obtain. Realistically they are.

All things being equal it is necessary that the price be right. If a prospective property is being offered at fair market value and contains any of the various options, then it is a natural for leverage. Apply the option that appears to fit best and determine if the application of the option enhances the value. Actually, I would suggest the application of all of the available options in order to check myself.

19

How To Cash In On The Amazing Condominium Bonanza

Condominium is the in-word in today's real estate industry. The ancient Romans built condominiums, but they were unknown in America 20 years ago, little known as recently as 15 years ago, yet very well known today. The popularity of the condominium surged because it coalesced the superiority of home owning with none of the problems of home repairs, landscaping, etc. It is possible to dwell in an apartment, enjoy the luxurious benefits of this type of living, and also take pleasure in the tax benefits available to home owners.

Condominium Tax Factors

The favorability of the condominiums started with retired people acquiring "second home apartments" in vacationlands throughout the country. Diverse by degree, this type of acquisition began being used by many tax-conscious people who were taking advantage of liberal government tax laws. Soon afterward a third group joined the other two groups. Fundamentally, this group may be described as those people who have decided that they would rather build up equity instead of saving worthless rent receipts.

Condominiums Aid Home Buying

Inflation, high construction costs, high land cost, and high interest rates have all combined to position one family homes out of range for many young people. Yet the condominiums have made it possible for these same people to purchase homes.

Recently married young couples have little use for one family homes. These one family units usually contain between six and nine rooms. The immediate need of newlyweds is between three and four rooms. What has been taking place is that the newlyweds have been acquiring smaller unit apartments at between $25,000 to $27,000. When the need arises for additional room the apartment is sold and with the added equity profit the young couple is now in a healthier financial position to purchase a $35,000 to $40,000 one family residence.

What Is A Condominium?

The meaning of a condominium is basically not elaborate. The apartment is purchased and owned by the individual. There is a deed and customarily a mortgage for each apartment. All of the public facilities, the hallways, land, etc. are owned in common by all of the apartment owners. Carrying charges are apportioned among the tenants. In order to secure easier running of buildings a governing board is selected by the tenants. The governing board, in turn, hires a management firm to manage the property.

The individual occupants may, whenever they desire, sell their apartment without seeking permission from any governing group. This provides for greater flexibility. Consequently, when the condominium owner needs a larger apartment or merely wants to receive a profit, he may do so without seeking permission from anyone else. The condominium owner is only restricted by the terms of the original sales agreement which generally has little or no sales restrictions.

The mortgage market for condominiums is excellent. The lenders are now interested in this type loan because F.H.A. guarantees are now available under section 234 of the National Housing Act. The mortgage applications, while not challenging single family dwellings, are increasing rapidly. The popularity of the condominiums appears to be increasing largely by word of mouth.

One of the prominent features of the condominiums is the social club. The club provides dances, card games, general socializing, etc. The club also ties in with the swimming and tennis facilities. The ability to meet all your neighbors rapidly is certainly a vast improvement over the old method of waiting neglected for your neighbor to introduce himself.

Very nearly all states have statutes regulating organization and operation of condominiums. These regulations are in many cases quite comprehensive. The items regulated in detail include:

(A) Detailed floor plans including sizes and layouts of each rental unit.

(B) Location, description of topography and description of development.

(C) Developers' mode of selling.

(D) Spelling out of fractional ownership interest of each apartment.

A short time back I was interested in a group developing a Florida condominium. The property involved was a well-located one family residence. The site was a remarkably good one, being within easy walking distance of strong local retail shopping. Municipal transportation was also close at hand. The other buildings in the immediate area are all four to six story properties; the use of buildings in the region was more or less evenly divided between superior apartment dwellings, better hotels and cooperative apartment buildings. The condominium had not yet made its appearance in this town. The average age of these properties was from 40 to 50 years. The individual building under examination was forty-two years old, not really old, but a well-built gracious building.

Condominium Cost!!

In spite of its many qualities the lovely one family residence was marked for demolition. The sponsors of the project prepared their analysis upon the following cost estimate.

(A)	Cost of land, 20,000 square feet at $10.00 a square foot	$ 200,000
(B)	Cost of improvement, to include apartments, pool, tennis courts, 1,500,000 cubic feet @ $2.00 per cubic foot	$3,000,000
(C)	Cost of parking and basement 190,000 cubic feet @ $1.50 per cubic foot	$ 285,000
(D)	Architect's and Engineering Fees	$ 125,000
(E)	Financing interim taxes	$ 65,000
(F)	Sponsors' profit	$ 300,000
(G)	Construction overhead	$ 100,000
(H)	Sales cost	$ 100,000
	Total Cost	$4,175,000

The Fantastic World Of Condominiums

The condominium proves itself to be a happy marriage. The sponsor turns a neat profit. The purchaser acquires a situation to his liking. The condominium love affair seems to be picking up steam and in the foreseeable future may possibly provide real competition for single family builders.

The extent of the condominium has not only affected high-rise apartment buildings but also garden apartments, beach clubs and shopping centers. Personally, I believe that it is only a matter of time before the condominium includes a new and possibly its most fantastic outlet—office buildings. It is entirely possible that every conceivable type of real estate will eventually fall under the spell of the condominium to its advantage.

Tax Authorities Love Condominiums

Condominiums are favorites of municipal taxing authorities, the reason being that all things being equal a condominium will yield greater revenues than apartment buildings. An associate of mine built an apartment building containing 150 three-room rental units. The proposed rental was to be $250 per month or $3,000 per annum. The total rent roll of the building was projected at $450,000 per annum. The taxing authorities would have based their taxes on a market valuation of six and one half times gross rental, or $2,925,000.

Condominiums Are Worth More

Due to the increasing demand for condominiums it was decided to change the project to a condominium. The fair market value for sales of units of this type was $28,000. The gross sales were estimated at $4,200,000. With a $4,200,000 property as against the alternate value of $2,925,000, the taxing authority preferred, because of increased revenue, the construction of condominiums.

Fabulous Financing Benefits

The condominium has another solid attraction for builders. Builders that I know prefer condominiums to rental units because of the fabulous financing benefits. Let us take a rental building erected two years ago. The building had a rent roll of $500,000. The market value was 6.5 times the gross rental—$3,250,000. The permanent mortgage 70% of valuation—$2,275,000.

Let us hypothecate the same job as a condominium. The market value of a condominium is, of course, the sum total of the sales price of each unit. The total sales would have been approximately $4,200,000. The permanent mortgage loan would run approximately 75% of value or $3,150,000.

In correlating the rental building as against the condominium, we found both jobs cost the same amount of money to build. The builder of the rental unit, however, would have to add about 20% to his mortgage in order to pay all the bills. So the cash outlay for the builder, in this instance, is $490,000, the true cost of the job being $2,940,000.

Now let us analyze the condominium position. This job also has a total cost of $2,940,000. However, with a mortgage loan of $3,150,000 the builder will mortgage out with a $210,000 profit. We now can determine that the difference between the two types of jobs is that the condominium builder lays out no money to build his job and in fact makes a profit. The leasing builder must lay out 20% of the job in cash.

The general consensus of many builders and brokers is that as long as the 75% mortgage is available to condominiums, apartment rentals remain high and condominiums remain competitive, their future is assured.

The condominium has become the deliverance for young married couples. The average young married couple is faced with the problem of securing a roof over their heads. The options are:

(A) Apartments that rent for more than most budgets can stand.

(B) One family homes that sell for between $40,000 and $50,000. The carrying costs will usually strangle a young family's budget.

(C) Condominiums that are available for between $20,000 to $25,000. Down payments that are within the family budget, usually $3,000 to $5,000.

The condominium price should, despite inflationary trends, continue to remain static. Some experts have predicted that by 1980 approximately 75% of all residential dwellings will be condominiums. With this expanded growth, competition should hold down price increases.

Among its attractive features the condominium offers a choice. The choice is large enough to satisfy most particularly on a temporary basis. The various types of condominiums are the following:

Garden Apartments
Town Houses
High-Rise Apartments

It is true that some condominium owners have not been altogether happy with their purchases. This is to be expected. However, with the exercise of prudent care much of the dissatisfaction may be eliminated. Some of the problems include management problems, understated expenses, and bad condominium contracts. Most problems can be eliminated or at least the purchaser may be made aware of them through the employment of a real estate attorney. A number of entrepreneurs shove their contracts down the throat of their purchasers. If your attorney suggests contract changes and the entrepreneurs refuse to make them, then the deal should be rejected. The most flagrant criticism falls upon the so-called recreational facilities clauses. A number of builders attempt to exclude the club rooms, pools, golf courses and tennis facilities. Instead of owning these facilities the condominium owners learn, too late, that they are only net leased and not owned. From this position a number of entrepreneurs have been able to milk substantial funds from the condominium owners.

One fact is obvious. The condominium is here to stay. How good a deal an individual purchaser makes is his, and his attorney's, decision.

What To Look For

Condominiums have the potential to become the greatest single force in the investment scheme of things. Condominiums have been established to embrace the following:

Office buildings	Warehousing centers
Apartment buildings	Storage centers
Industrial complexes	Golf courses
Commercial centers	Trailer parks

As you can see the condominium field is vast in scope. In order to make money with condominiums you must pick the type that appeals most, and create a condominium in this field. One of the underlying principals of real estate is that "a user will always pay more." This principal is utilized in your creation of a condominium. Look for a property that is enhanced by an aura of pride of ownership. This is best applied to residential properties. If your choice is a commercial or industrial condominium then the secret is to secure a building tenanted with occupancy that is "doing well."

To sum up: It is far more profitable to sell a parcel in pieces than to sell a property as a whole entity.

20

Tremendous Profits Through Run-Down Buildings

Any time we examine run-down buildings we are discussing both small and large apartment buildings. For the most part the occupancy is composed of low income families. The areas where these buildings predominate are usually called "ghettos."

Within any large city, the community with a low income level will be found residing in pre-1920 buildings. Hypothetically there is a continuous hostility between the tenant and the landlord. However, I must point out that in many cases this is pure nonsense. In order to continue collecting rents from a tenement, it is necessary to properly maintain the property. A landlord who does not properly preserve his building will lose the building.

With buildings of more recent vintage it is possible to avoid numerous repairs and not find yourself in a catastrophic position. However, the great extent of low-rent dwellings are very ancient buildings—some being nearly 100 years old. If an ancient building is neglected it will deteriorate far more rapidly than a building of more recent origin and so it does need constant attention.

An analysis of a dilapidated apartment building's profit and loss statement reveals that the average building will show a profit of 50%, before deducting an expense item for repairs. In order to maintain a static level, 25% must be allocated to repairs. This, of course, leaves 25% as a cash flow, the cash flow being the net profit achieved after the payment of all expenses including interest and amortization.

Government Money Needed For Upgrading

In order to maintain proper upkeep and to gradually modernize and improve a run-down property it is necessary to use approximately 50% of the gross rental income as a repair expense. This means that in order to maintain and modernize such buildings, a landlord must be prepared to lose money. It is not rational to expect a private investor to buy a building for the purpose of losing money. Possibly the answer lies in several directions:

- (A) Municipal ownership of tenements and upgrading of properties through governmental subsidy.
- (B) Municipal ownership of tenements, followed by demolition and erection of new subsidized rental units.
- (C) A combination of both A and B.

Ghetto Patterns

I have had many encounters with the ownership of pre-1920 buildings. I have had ample opportunity to examine the degeneration of neighborhoods. The history of low-income neighborhoods is a transition of groups according to wealth. The rotation of economic groups begins with the wealthy and slowly works its way down to welfare occupancy. A bit of incidental information to this rotation is that these regions are inhabited by many different racial groups. As the areas change in aggregate qualities so do the ethnic groups. There is no ordained pattern—in affluent neighborhoods you will discover Jewish, Irish, Italian, Negro and other groups. On the other hand, these same assemblages may be located in middle class and in "ghetto" neighborhoods. When one group leaves a locality another moves in.

Owning and managing a run-down building is unlike ownership of other realty. I recall that at the time I purchased my first, I was of the opinion that the cash flow profit was copious enough for me to start rehabilitating the property.

Understanding Neighborhoods

I was resolute to start my rehabilitation program with the lobby. The front door was missing and the plaster walls had numerous holes. I ordered a maintenance company to install a new front door, spackle and paint, and in general clean up the lobby. The work was completed and I surveyed the results with a great sense of personal pride. I had a sensation of "Super Landlord." I had achieved work above and beyond the call of a landlord's obligation.

Two weeks later I informally visited the building to view closely my pride and joy—the lobby. Wow! It appeared as if a hurricane had hit the lobby. The new front door was gone and the numerous holes in the lobby walls had reappeared.

The building department files violations against buildings in this condition. Newspapers run large exposés of these buildings and liberally toss about the term "slumlord." Tenants' organizations raise much flak and attract political pressure.

I received much of this abuse and the only satisfaction that I achieved came from knowing that I did the very best that I could. I supplied every reasonable service and prevented further decay of the buildings. In addition I took heart in knowing that sometime within the next few years a change for the best must take place. If governmental subsidies are not forthcoming then a large segment of the city will devour itself. The rate of abandoned buildings will increase to the point that the development of urban communities will come to a screeching halt.

Managing Agents Needed In Ghetto Areas

I purchased my first run-down property along Seventh Avenue in New York. This building provided me with much experience in the operation of this distinctive type property. I learned that it is most important to engage a managing agent. The managing agent serves as a shock absorbing apparatus between the landlord and the very real, physical ghetto.

At the time that I acquired my first building I immediately ran into difficulty. I was unable to obtain liability insurance. My insurance broker tried every available company with no luck. How was I going to protect myself with liability insurance? I eventually came up with what I felt was a unique solution. The property was held in a corporate name with no personal liability. There was a first mortgage lien against the property. In order to protect myself against a large liability claim, through a business associate I placed a $200,000 second mortgage against the property. In the event of a large liability award the second mortgage would have to be satisfied in order to take over the property. If anyone wished to satisfy the second mortgage I was perfectly content to receive $200,000, which was considerably more than the property was worth.

Use A Managing Agent—It's Cheaper

Numerous investors are working full time in some field other than real estate: doctors, attorneys, and executives. They generally are persons with some knowledge of real estate. These investors are, in the main, unfamiliar with these type properties but are intrigued with the stories of pecuniary gain. However, this group of investors have a common problem—time or lack of it. They would love to participate in the large profits, but cannot take time away from their primary vocations.

The unsophisticated answer to this problem is to hire a managing agent. However, this is an oversimplification. Run-down properties are vastly different from other types of real estate and so have particular regulations. Managing agents are available at fees of between 3% to 10% of the gross rental. This type property has this management fee spread depending upon location. The healthier locations command lower fees and conversely the "tough" neighborhoods command higher fees. When determining your management fee, check the neighborhood—it is your barometer.

Can you run a run-down property without a management agent? Of course you can. But you must have the available time. A thirty family building will require about four hours a week to run properly. In some areas, where there is rent control, the time element is much greater. In areas like New York City the paper work is heavy. In "Welfare Buildings" many municipalities throughout the country require a substantial amount of paper work. It can be stated that such a place may require between 4-8 hours per week depending on tenancy and location.

Figure Necessary Repairs In Advance

An additional matter sometimes overlooked by even experienced investors is the initial cost of repairs. This is an extremely important item as it may easily add 10% additional cash investment to the agreed upon purchase price. The principal items to be checked are as follows:

- (A) Roof
- (B) Plumbing
- (C) Dry rot in wood
- (D) Structural defects
  - (1) Beams
  - (2) Walls
  - (3) Foundations
- (E) Heating, including boiler

There are a considerable number of engineering and inspection firms that specialize in "Pre-Purchase Inspection" reports. In utilizing this type of service you may ascertain any additional cash outlays in which you may become involved. The costs will vary depending upon the individual firms, but it does not entail great expense and certainly is worthwhile.

At the time that you acquire an older building you will have to live with the property. Indeed, even if you have a managing agent you will, to a degree, be involved. I fervently urge any prospective purchaser to inquire if the present tenants are happy and satisfied. Bear in mind that more money may be assured with happy tenants than with dissatisfied tenants. In this type property, a single, active dissatisfied tenant may cause numerous difficulties. I urge going from door to door and engaging in conversation with each tenant. I am aware that many investors avoid this system, asserting that it may "open a Pandora's Box." If there are a large number of complaints from many tenants then you should not purchase the property.

Landlords Are Good Guys Too

Landlords are not completely sinners—quite often they are sinned against. Many municipalities across the nation have laws that may be taken advantage of by unscrupulous tenants. If the tenant can convince an inspector that a repair has not been done, he may have his rent reduced by a judge. What some tenants do is to deliberately cause damage to their apartment. After the landlord makes his repair it is promptly sabotaged. When the building inspector arrives he finds that the work has not been done. The landlord may be fined and the tenant's rent reduced.

As far as unscrupulous tenants are concerned, they may be beaten at their own game. To begin with, there is almost never more than a single unscrupulous tenant to a building. When a repair is made it should be dated, described and witnessed by the contractor and a notary public. This procedure is only necessary when you do run into the troublesome or cheating tenant.

Despite the many problems involved, run-down buildings make good investments. If you have the time and can cope with various situations that may arise then you should not have any concern about purchasing such a building. Run-down properties throw off a good profit and you should take advantage of this type investment.

What To Look For

Old buildings, particularly old run-down buildings, lack eye appeal. This eye appeal, sometimes called pride of ownership, turns off many potential buyers. When a group of buyers will not bid for a property the exposure is reduced and the value of the property drops. This action tends to increase yields on equity. Look for buildings that are unattractive in looks but that have all the other characteristics of a good purchase.

There are certain times when properties in this group may be purchased at great bargains. When the media stress the poor condition of such buildings and inflate area social problems, these properties become excellent buys because the prices drop even further.

When seeking your building try for one that has only a first mortgage. In many old neighborhoods, it is difficult, impossible or very expensive to get liability insurance. To counteract this situation many owners place large second mortgages against their properties. The holder of the mortgage may be your mother, father, wife, child, etc. The amount of the second mortgage should be large enough to cover your investment. The mortgage will serve as a buffer against any possible liability claims. To further reduce your liability the property should be purchased in a corporate name.

21

How To Find Hidden Bargains In Retail Drive-Ins

To fully understand the economic importance of the drive-in retail store we must go back to the 1950's. During this period drive-in retail units were composed chiefly of gasoline stations, soft ice cream stands and some fast food hamburger stands. Subsequently both progress and inflation took over. The gasoline stations converted from small two bay stations to large super service stations. The soft ice cream units gradually gave up their drive-ins as the rent became too costly and forced them to divert their operation to stores. The individual hamburger stands were subsequently replaced by large multimillion dollar chains.

Numerous real estate people think the drive-in scene has become the most rapidly growing segment of the industry.

Drive-Ins A Major Industry

To give you an idea of how much is involved in the drive-in field, I will list the various types of businesses involved. The list, while large, is not complete, because it continues to grow.

Supermarkets	Donuts
Restaurants	Service Stations
Furniture	Paint
Steak Houses	Shoes
Fast Foods	Superettes
Department Stores	Appliances
Tire, Battery & Accessory	Fabric
Film Developing	Clothing
Dry Cleaning	Drug
Soft Ice Cream	Car Wash

Home Improvement

Drive-Ins A Major Category

As a major real estate category the drive-in involves many hundreds of millions of dollars. Most transactions consist of four segments:

(A) The builder
(B) The chain that guarantees the lease
(C) The franchisee
(D) The purchaser of the package

The role of each is fairly obvious. The builder builds the structure according to specifications furnished by the chain. The land may be either purchased or leased. The chain signs a long term lease, then sub-leases to the franchisee. The chain, however, remains primarily liable. In most cases the entire package is purchased by an investor.

The period since the early sixties has been an interesting one for the real estate investment world. Much of this interest has been created by chain and franchise drive-in firms. Some of them are pure chains, that is, those companies owning and operating their own retail units. The so-called franchise firm, on the other hand, is in most cases not pure because a number of them operate both their own retail units and franchise units. A number of the franchise units managed to stay alive, not through doing business, but through selling franchises. When the franchise market appeared to be slowing down a sales gimmick was brought into use. Companies sold "geography," that was, the granting of statewide and area distributorships. But this too reached a saturation point. When these companies realized that they were in trouble—their only income being the proceeds from franchise and stock sales—they stopped using gimmicks and tried learning to make money through the operation of their business. Some of the firms were immediately successful while others failed. Still others were plagued with growing pains in the form of temporary losses.

Franchise Gimmicks

As the years progressed, a good number of these chains gained strength, and actually became strong AAA-1 companies. However, some of them had a problem. Franchisees were either hard to come by, or they could not wait six months for a unit to be erected. As a solution, the franchise firms bought and built their own real estate and only secured an operator when the unit was open. Now an additional problem was created. Vast sums of money were needed to finance these ventures. The mortgage market was poor and consequently money was not available. Still another gimmick was brought into play, the sale-leaseback. This time the "gimmick" was a good one. The firms sold and leased back their own real estate. The arrangement worked admirably for both the companies and the investors. Once again a little gremlin "gimmick" had come to the rescue.

Certain drive-in companies decided that it would be nice to sell their properties but still derive important ownership advantages. Impossible? Don't believe it. Nothing is impossible with the gimmick-oriented minds of second assistant vice-presidents of some drive-in firms. Some of these firms decided that they should have repurchase options, the result being in some cases that of the purchaser lending money at rates lower than bank rates. Another problem for the purchaser was how the Federal government would treat his depreciation. Was the transaction a sale or was it merely lending money? Were some of the drive-in firms finished? Not by a long shot. The worst gimmick of all, for the purchaser, was introduced. Drive-in firms insisted upon repurchase options at less money than the original purchase price.

The professional real estate investor who has helped many of these gimmick oriented firms survive is being forced to the sidelines because of the difficult deals presented. Gimmicks are novelties and they generally survive for a short time and then wither away. The firms interested solely in cute, gimmick-type deals may awaken to find that professionals want no part of them. And part time owners will surely follow suit. These actions could hurt the drive-in firms badly. Many of them seem to be in need of top real estate consultants who can structure palatable transactions.

How To Buy Franchise Real Estate

There are many fine, well-rated drive-in firms offering agreeable deals to the public. The rate of return will vary slightly, depending upon the prime rate. It is safe to figure points over the prime rate for blue-chip firms. The rate goes up for firms with a lesser degree of financial strength. Blue-chip firms are purchased for less than prime rate and almost always are sold on a free and clear basis, because financing would decrease the yield.

The packages sold today run from $60,000 to $450,000 with the cost of building and land about equally divided. Further, with the present expensive money, 95% of these transactions are on a free and clear basis. Yields are generally as follows:

(A) Companies with net worth to one million dollars, 2½–3 points over prime rate.

(B) Companies with net worth to fifteen million dollars, two points over prime rate.

(C) Companies with net worth to seventy-five million dollars, prime rate to one point over prime rate.

(D) Companies with net worth over seventy-five million dollars, minus one point over prime rate.

The aforementioned schedule applies to investors who are delivered a complete package. Builders receive an additional 2–4% as their building fee. The lease must be a true net lease. Operators purchasing large numbers of units gain 1–1½% over the norm. Where the lease is not fully net—say the landlord is responsible for structural repairs—then the yield will be 1–1½% more than the scheduled rates.

I personally believe that companies providing gimmick-free leases will do well in a highly competitive market for their real estate.

A great many of the drive-in investments are offered as package deals. The investor purchases the land, a lease and specifications for a building to be built or the deal is offered with an older building to be remodeled.

New buildings offer greater values than older buildings. If you purchase or construct a new drive-in property for the amounts you would spend to purchase an older drive-in and modernize it, the modernization is a poor risk. I make this statement based upon many actual deals that I have observed.

Does Remodeling Pay?

In order to create a ratio of a new drive-in department store as against an old building plus modernization, I will offer a hypothetical situation based upon today's real estate market. I do not suggest that this particular situation will prevail in all instances, but rather that it will occur often enough to be of importance.

As an example I will illustrate a brand new drive-in type department store of 200,000 square feet of store space. A building of that type could be constructed for approximately twenty-five dollars per square foot. The space would rent for $8.50 per square foot, including overages. An analysis of the investment is as follows:

Total Investment

Building	$5,000,000
Land	300,000
Total	$5,300,000
Mortgage (75%)	3,950,000
Cash Equity	$1,350,000

Profit and Loss Statement

Income	$1,700,000
Expenses	1,125,000
Net Income	$ 575,000
Interest & amortization	$ 397,500
Net Return	$ 177,500
Return on Equity	13.1%

Now compare an older drive-in department store of the same size and similar location.

A building of advanced age would undoubtedly suffer from economic obsolescence. There would be no mall, limited parking, and probably no opportunity for overages because of competition from newer units with better facilities. Actually jobs of this type may have the last vestiges of overages, which rapidly disappear to the formidable competition of newer buildings.

To compete on an equal basis, the older drive-in would require a complete modernization which might include a mall, parking lot repairs and new lighting, new air-conditioning, recessed fluorescent lighting, new flooring, acoustical ceilings, decorating and modernization of store fronts.

The total investment could easily come to $5.00 a square foot or $1,000,000. The investment analysis could be as follows:

Cost of Building and Land

Purchase Price (six times income)	$4,800,000
Modernization	1,000,000
Total Invested	$5,800,000
Mortgage (2/3 of value)	3,866,667
Cash Equity	$1,933,333

Income:

($4.00 sq. ft. including overages)	$ 800,000
Expenses	400,000
Net Income	$ 400,000
Interest & amortization	320,000
Cash Flow	$ 80,000
Return on Equity:	4% plus/minus

The expensive result of the modernization is to create a return on equity of approximately 4%. While the modernization may serve to increase rentals, it also means a waiting time until leases expire. If the existing lease is long-term, then there is little future in the property.

Failure to modernize could mean a good profit in the beginning but a gradual scaling down of profits as newer retail units gradually gather strength—a strength that comes from the older jobs and surely robs them of economic life.

Drive-ins, of course, must also be approached from another angle—the smaller unit situations of 2,500′ to 10,000′ on plots varying from 10,000′ to three acres. The smaller drive-ins are sold fully completed to investors.

Franchise Problems

During the sixties many new drive-in companies were formed and many of these companies had financial difficulties. Basically these problems were caused by:

      (A) Under financing
      (B) Inexperience and mismanagement
      (C) Over-expansion

To be more explicit, new companies were formed, went public and became sound financially. This situation dissipated, however, through wild expansion. Companies that should have been opening five to six new locations a year were opening fifty to sixty locations a year. Management that had been able to handle perhaps a dozen units was now attempting to operate one hundred units. Numerous new companies were not equal to the task. It's a situation that is not unusual in new fields that suddenly mushroom. There is generally a shaking out period for those who cannot shape up. Weak companies go under while better managed and stronger firms prosper and grow larger.

"Buy fast food drive-in restaurants." Does this statement sound like financial disaster? Don't believe it. There is a solid, growing need for drive-in restaurants that may take twenty years or more to catch up with demand. Firms that had financial problems were suffering financially, but not from a lack of business.

I have found many investors backing off when drive-in restaurants were mentioned. Real estate wise, the most effective method for changing styles and trends is public opinion. To a great degree public opinion is pliable, and as a consequence sometimes easily molded. Word of mouth images are built slowly and steadily until they are presumed Gospel. However, I now believe that the industry is at long last beginning to realize that those firms which prevailed, after the initial fast food shake-up, are strong growing companies—companies with money, experience and top personnel.

As with all investments there is a risk factor. However, this factor can be reduced to a minimum. Before entertaining the idea of the purchase of a fast food drive-in you should ask some pertinent questions and have your accountant, lawyer or real estate broker secure the answers.

How long has the company been in business? The minimum answer to this is at least ten years. Has the company been making money? The answer must be yes. The really good companies, particularly during inflationary periods, increase their earnings each and every year. Be very careful when analyzing a company's financial statement. There are many deceptive ways of preparing a statement. I would strongly urge having an accountant check all statements.

The upper 25% of the drive-in food chains are reasonably safe investments. There appears to be little in the foreseeable future that can prove this statement wrong. The fast food chains, the stronger ones, have proven that they can cope with inflationary trends and still prosper.

Buying Second Line Companies

Certain investors are of the opinion that they can purchase "second line" drive-in restaurants and be just as safe as those investors who purchase quality chains. The reasoning behind this thinking is that an astute investor may make his investment as good as an AAA-1 one by purchasing a drive-in restaurant situated at a superior location. I do not doubt that a reasonably experienced real estate investor may identify a 100% location as against say a 60% location. I also admit that a 100% location will create far more business than a 60% location. Here, however, is where truth replaces hope. The 100% location may do a tremendous amount of business and still not make money. On the other hand a 60% location, with a much lower rental may also lose money, because of poor business. The moral is that the only way to be sure of minimum risk is to buy paper. That is, make sure that the lease is with a quality company. Quality companies offer smaller yields but the investment is infinitely safer.

The harsh truth about marginal firms is that even if you pick a tremendous location at a reasonable rental you can still be a loser. The company itself may go bankrupt, thereby causing financial problems for all its landlords. On the other hand a quality company may be installed at a poor location and even though business may be bad the chain will in all probability remain a good financial risk for the landlord.

Real estate is a fanciful business which has the ability to make improbable dreams come true. You may find remarkable bargains just waiting to be picked up. I recall a deal that was made several years ago on the east coast. A client was seeking a small investment parcel in Florida. His choice was either Miami or Jacksonville. The final choice was Jacksonville. Back in the forties one of the main Jacksonville shopping streets was able to command $500 to $600 per front foot. The traffic count thirty years later was about 30,000 cars as against about 20,000 cars in the forties. Despite the 30 year inflationary trend and the high traffic count, rentals had dropped. The particular parcel that was under consideration was one badly damaged by fire, caused by old wiring. The property was in a poor retail area. The building itself had previously been used as a gas station. It was not in the 100% business block, but close to the 100% area. In fact the property was three long blocks from the center of the action. The owner was of a mind to collect his money from the insurance company, sell the real estate and run from the area before values decreased additionally.

My client was aware of the value of fringe properties with good traffic counts and wanted to own this real estate. The previous tenant had paid $10,000 per annum and struggled to pay his rent. The tenant's problem stemmed from the wrong type of business being in the right location.

I was asked to help with the purchase of the property. I talked with the landlord and learned that he was interested in selling at a price of $50,000 all cash. My client did not have $50,000, but rather than admit defeat I went to work trying to put together a deal.

I approached a few drive-in restaurant chains and eventually one responded affirmatively. The other chains rejected the area because it was "out of the action." They clearly neglected to consider the excellent traffic count. The chain interested in the location offered to pay $20,000 per annum net net net for twenty years, the only hitch being that they wanted the building repaired and altered to their specifications. The cost would run to $30,000. I began to smell the makings of a deal.

Negotiations commenced and I offered the landlord $15,000 per annum net net net for 20 years, if he would spend the $30,000 needed to alter and renovate the property. The landlord, over the term of the lease, would be getting an additional $100,000 and his net profit would be $270,000 over the term of the lease, plus still retaining ownership of the property. I arranged for a twenty year lease with the landlord and simultaneously signed a lease with the restaurant chain, which was subleasing from my client. The owner was aware of my negotiations with the chain at all times.

The deal was beautiful for everyone. The landlord would net $270,000 instead of selling the property for $50,000. The restaurant chain was delighted with the location—a real money maker. I made a nice brokerage commission. My client subleased for $20,000 per annum for twenty years, or a total of $100,000. He had absolutely no investment except my leasing commission. If you want to work at it, "sleeper" properties may be controlled with little or no investment. The greatest opportunity would appear to be in the drive-in field. There are many sites that appear to be weak, but actually have very good traffic counts. A smart operator can pick up these properties at bargain prices.

What To Look For

In purchasing a drive-in it is important to look for certain physical characteristics that will aid in providing a sound base for your investment. First, do not purchase a property unless it has a minimum plot of 20,000 square feet. If the occasion should arise whereby it is necessary to secure a new tenant, today's drive-in tenancy requirements practically make a 20,000 square foot plot mandatory. The smaller plots are no longer economically feasible.

Another important physical characteristic is the layout of the improvement. In checking out a prospective purchase look for a multi-purpose building. Again, we require this type of building as security in the event of a tenant change.

When looking for a drive-in, net leased purchase make sure that you do not find yourself locked in. The tenant's lease should contain cost of living increases. During a period of recession, with high interest rates, the property value may erode.

22

How To Make Money With Land

In the previous chapters I have examined improved property investments. Now I intend to go into unimproved property—vacant land. An oversimplified view of land is that there is only a specified amount of available land and additional quantities cannot be produced. Therefore, the value of land increases as it decreases in size. This theory carries with it the assumption that eventually all unimproved land will vanish. If this were true, buying land would be one of the least difficult forms of profitable investment. Actually, this theory is not true. Many parcels are used over and over.

Land May Be Recycled

Many years ago a refugee disembarked from an ocean liner in New York City. For a time this man worked in New York City in the building trade. When he had saved some money he decided to become a builder. He began small and gradually became an important builder. Much of his construction was confined to an upper middle class area in New York City. For many years this man continued building. During the ensuing years the business was turned over to the next generation. At this point all of the land in this urban community had been built. This fact did not retard the new generation of builders. Old apartment buildings were torn down and replaced by new, modern office buildings. This is interesting in that it contradicts the story about running out of land. We are also reminded that prime land locations may be used many times, while poor locations may be avoided completely by developers.

In the same area, another firm of developers did the identical thing. They demolished apartment buildings built many years before, and replaced them with larger apartment buildings. I mention both firms only to illustrate that it is not unusual, nor unique, to recycle land. In big cities land is constantly reused. The Federal Government also reuses land. The Housing Act of 1949, an urban renewal program, has served as the vehicle that helped clear slums and replace them with modern housing, industrials and commercial properties. In effect land is reused.

The vacant land actually available in this country is rather a large quantity—some two billion acres. Estimates on the value of this land run as high as 850 billion dollars. Estimates show an overall average of vacant land in this country to have an appreciation of 42½ billion per annum, a 5% yearly appreciation.

Land buying and selling is a fascinating business. Strangely, there has been far more money made in vacant land than in improved properties. When investors purchase an improved property they are interested primarily in the amount of cash to be invested, the return on equity and the safety factor. I have perceived these same prudent people unexpectedly change into uninhibited gamblers when acquiring land. These people see a parcel, like the parcel and buy it. When you inquire why they bought this particular parcel the answer invariably is "land always goes up." This type of reasoning is absolutely wrong. Nevertheless, during the 50's, 60's and 70's the incorrect method of buying actually worked. This is, however, no guarantee that land prices will continue to spiral upward at an accelerating pace.

Leverage With Land

One of the more irresistible aspects of land speculation is that it creates tremendous leverage. An automobile salesman I know decided to take a flyer and purchased a piece of land for $20,000. Actual cash put up was $5,000, with the balance being a mortgage. Within six months the property was sold for $40,000. What was the profit? $20,000? Absolutely not. Only $5,000 cash was put up. The property was sold for $40,000 with all cash above the $15,000 mortgage; the new purchaser paying $25,000 cash of which $20,000 was profit. In this instance a profit of 400% was made within six months. It is these fantastic profits that cause the land excitement.

The Land Purchase Formula

Real estate land acquisition is actually a scientific business guided by formula. The process is reasonably simple and highly effective. The formula is as follows:

Cost:
Land	$	
Building		
Carrying Charges		
Misc.	_____	
Total Cost	$	
Mortgage (−)	_____	
Cash In Job	$	

Estimated Rent Roll	$
Expenses: (−)	_____
Cash Flow	$

The above captioned formula is a simple procedure that will determine if the project contemplated is feasible or in it simplest form provides the answer to the land value. In order to conclude a proposed project on paper: First, the highest and best use for the property is determined. Then the total cost of the project is arrived at by totalling the land cost, building cost, carrying charges and miscellaneous expenses. From this total a proposed mortgage is subtracted. This gives the amount of cash left in the job. Next we estimate a rent roll and list all operating expenses. The operating cost is subtracted from the estimated rent roll and we arrive at an estimated cash flow. Then by dividing the cash equity into the cash flow we arrive at the percentage yield. The yield should be three points above those used to determine fair market value for improved properties.

If all of your estimates are correct and the percentage yield is correct, then the land price is correct. If the percentage yield is higher than fair market value then the land is priced below market and is a good buy. Conversely, if the percentage yield is low then the land is overpriced. Do not buy land because you feel that it will go up in price. This is too fragile a justification upon which to invest hard earned money.

If an investor has a conviction that he must speculate then I suppose that I must help by revealing the secret system used by Elmer R., a well known land speculator. Elmer would begin by carefully selecting a town in which to operate. The town had to be a booming town—one that was having a substantial amount of residential growth. After the town is picked out, Elmer will purchase a number of vacant parcels along the fringe of the town. Great care is taken to make sure that the parcels purchased are in the path of progress.

What makes this system absolutely ingenious is the simple, but effective, method of purchase. Rather than acquire one sizable parcel, Elmer prefers to purchase ten parcels. The usual cash equity is 5% of the purchase price, the balance being a mortgage. In the beginning of his operation Elmer sells off parcels for small profits with the excess proceeds going to reduce the mortgages on the remaining properties. The manner in which it customarily works is that the last parcel or sometimes the last few parcels are paid in full with the profits of the earlier sales. Once Elmer has his money back he is in a position to hold the remaining properties until he achieves the highest available price.

Another land speculator that I know had a unique system for land speculation. This chap, an accountant by trade, goes into farm country to purchase his land. The accountant's main preference is for farms with large frontages on main highways. If suitable a farm is then purchased with approximately 25% down and the balance on a mortgage, the farm is then net leased back to the farmer. The farmer's rental covers taxes and mortgage payments. The accountant is now able to carry the property expense free. In order to enable himself to be able to sell within a reasonable time the lease with farmer will contain a cancellation clause. The leases are cancellable at the lessor's option at the end of any harvest.

The number of people who have disregarded all the rules and still managed to make substantial amounts of money through the buying of land is almost endless. All through the history of our country it has been land that has enabled people to amass great wealth. A classic is the story of Leon G. Leon was a small local builder engaged in building one and two family homes in Astoria, New York during the late 1930's. Leon was approached by a broker who offered to sell him some land, in fact several square blocks of land. Part of the land was zoned for business, while the balance was zoned for apartment buildings. Leon inquired about the price and the broker replied, "$5,000." Leon, for some strange reason, said "O.K. it's a deal." The broker advised Leon that the property was part of an estate and the offer would have to be approved by the court. The offer was submitted by telephone to the judge who requested a meeting the next day. Upon leaving the broker Leon began to think about his offer. What had he really offered? $5,000 was too much for a lot. On the other hand $5,000 was too little for a square block. Leon decided to play it cool and wait for the meeting at which time he would "play it by ear." That night Leon had little sleep. Finally, the next day dawned and with it the meeting with the judge. Promptly, at the appointed time, Leon was shown into the judge's chambers where the judge and the real estate broker were waiting. After an exchange of pleasantries the judge announced that the offer of $5,000 was acceptable. Now Leon was really worried. Was he buying a bargain? Was he overpaying drastically? Trying not to let his confusion show Leon asked to study the contract in order to check the terms. He quickly looked to the price and happily discovered that price was $5,000 per square block.

Leon purchased the property, which was four square city blocks for $20,000. Almost coincidentally there was a tremendous surge of building in Astoria. The area had good transportation in the form of buses and subways. Also, adjacent to Astoria was Long Island City with its many plants supplying work for the Astoria residents. The four blocks became almost priceless. Despite many tremendous offers Leon never sold. Over a period of years he built all of the parcels. Leon became a millionaire.

I do not recommend gambling, but if you must gamble do it with land. For some unknown reason Dame Fortune loves to smile upon land gamblers. To qualify my statement—to me a land gambler is someone who buys without logic, reason or formula. Many of these gamblers have been fantastically successful.

Land Luck

Possibly a classic example of "Land Luck," buying land indiscriminately and making a fortune at it is Big Harry. Harry worked for many years as a carpenter, decided that he could do better as a land speculator and bought some land. Harry has become a multi-millionaire.

When Harry drives about in his car his secretary Hilda sits at his side. Hilda must be ready in case Harry sees a parcel that he likes. The usual conversation is as follows:

> Harry: "That's a nice piece of land. Look in the book, Hilda, and see if I own it."

Hilda will check to see if Harry owns the land. If not, he will dispatch a real estate broker to purchase the property at the lowest possible price. Harry now owns so much land that he cannot recall from memory exactly which properties he owns.

I often wonder if people like Harry are merely lucky or if they have a natural instinct for seeking out good land buys. I believe that just as people have an ear for music, so other people must have an ear for land.

Land For $5.00 Per Acre

If you do not have big money to buy choice land parcels or if you wish to spread your money over a great many parcels, you can do so. There are thousands of acres of public lands available. The bulk of these lands are located in the western sectors of our nation. California lands are available at only $5.00 per acre minimum bid. The balance of the western states having available land include:

Arizona	New Mexico
Colorado	Oregon
Idaho	Utah
Montana	Washington
Nevada	Wyoming
	Alaska

The majority of western states have land available at $8-$10 per acre. As an American citizen you are entitled to bid for these properties. In 1938, the Congress of the United States passed an act which made it possible for citizens to obtain up to five acres for their own use. It is not necessary to farm these properties as was true under the Homestead Act. The lands may be used for recreation, homes, business, etc. Possibly 10% of all the land in the United States is available under the Small Tract Act.

The oil and gas lottery presents another opportunity to gamble for high stakes with small money. Here is how it works: From a government list you choose a property that interests you. You pay $10.00 for the parcel and fifty cents per acre for the oil and gas rights for one year. The winners are chosen by a lottery system. If you are not selected your money is returned. The percentage of people who have "hit it rich" with their oil and gas leases has been unbelievably high.

Land Bargains

Another source of land bargains is the U.S. National Forests. If you are looking for a nice summer retreat it is not necessary to pay high prices. The Federal Government has lots for lease. Some parcels may be leased for as little as $35.00 per year. Yes, you may build summer homes on the property.

Another source of "good buys" in vacant land can be found in the various auctions held for tax arrear properties. These auctions are held yearly by municipalities having tax powers. Brief descriptions of the available properties are advertised in local newspapers.

Participating in an auction is a tricky venture. People usually make up their minds in advance as to which property they prefer and how much they intend to pay for the parcel. Unfortunately, once the action begins for some people a spirit of competitiveness enters. After the limit previously decided upon is reached some people become angry and continue bidding. When several people react in this fashion the bidding becomes furious and the final prices ridiculous. It is imperative that a prospective bidder decide upon a final bid before entering the auction. He must discipline himself not to go beyond his original determination. If you are outbidded, then forget the property. If the next bidder feels that he can pay more than you—wish him luck.

Land to me has always had a special meaning. To me, vacant land presents a creative opportunity. A builder has the opportunity to not only create an investment opportunity, but also to create a work to benefit man. The profit motive is always present, but in conjunction there is the opportunity to help others.

Land For Community Betterment

An interesting situation developed several years ago. Harry R., an extremely wealthy builder, had his secretary call and command me to appear at his office the next day. I say command because Harry never asked, he always issued a command. Generally I avoided Harry, because he is the cheapest man I have ever known. I was curious and so I arrived at the appointed time. Harry informed me that he was going to build a development for elderly people. He intended to build the project without any government monies. I was commissioned to seek out an adequate site.

After considerable searching I located what I believed to be a choice parcel. The property was three acres in size, had a magnificent view of a large bay, was rustic and most important it was adjacent to a bus stop. The bus ride to the downtown city area was only fifteen minutes. In addition, the city fathers had seen fit to allow free bus rides for senior citizens.

I submitted the site to Harry. As expected he balked at the price. After considerable dickering with the owner, Harry purchased the property. A beautiful, luxury apartment building was built. The building contained a swimming pool, sauna baths, card rooms, a beautiful park and many other amenities. The project was truly superb. Actually, it seemed to be a country club for senior citizens. Frankly, I couldn't see how Harry could make money on the project.

Some months after the project was completed I learned the full story. Harry's mother, an elderly widow, had been installed in a luxury apartment building. Because the other tenants were of a different generation Harry's mother was unable to make friends. Within a year after the death of her husband the elderly lady died. Harry was shaken, believing that his mother had died of loneliness. Harry decided to try to help other senior citizens and the project was his contribution. A million dollar facility now stands as one man's contribution to his fellow man.

What To Look For

When contemplating the purchase of unimproved land there is one rule that absolutely must be observed—look into the topography.

Most urban areas, and many suburban areas, have good topography maps that will give a good general idea of the existing ground conditions. The topography maps only are to be used as a guide, because specific conditions can only be secured by having borings taken.

The importance of the topography maps and borings is that they serve to indicate if additional monies must be spent because of bad ground conditions. The additional monies to be spent should be deducted from what is determined to be a fair price for good land.

Another expense item that must be calculated is demolition. When purchasing a parcel with an improvement always get a demolition estimate. These demolition costs must be figured into the overall land cost.

Don't purchase in troubled sectors. Before making a commitment carefully look the area over for tell tale signs—vacant stores, vacant apartments, etc.

Index

Index